WHEN PARENTS DIE

WHEN PARENTS DIE

A GUIDE FOR ADULTS

EDWARD MYERS

◆ ◆ ◆

VIKING

VIKING
Viking Penguin Inc., 40 West 23rd Street,
New York, New York 10010, U.S.A.
Penguin Books Ltd, Harmondsworth,
Middlesex, England
Penguin Books Australia Ltd, Ringwood,
Victoria, Australia
Penguin Books Canada Limited, 2801 John Street,
Markham, Ontario, Canada L3R 1B4
Penguin Books (N.Z.) Ltd, 182–190 Wairau Road,
Auckland 10, New Zealand

First published in 1986 by Viking Penguin Inc.
Published simultaneously in Canada

Grateful acknowledgment is made for permission to reprint excerpts from the
following publications:
The Anatomy of Bereavement by Beverley Raphael. Copyright © 1983 by Professor
Beverley Raphael. Reprinted by permission of Basic Books, Inc., Publishers.
Attachment and Loss, Vol. 3: Loss by John Bowlby. Copyright © 1980 by The
Tavistock Institute of Human Relations. Reprinted by permission of Basic Books,
Inc., Publishers.
Recovery from Bereavement by Colin Murray Parkes and Robert S. Weiss. Copyright
© 1983 by Colin Murray Parkes and Robert S. Weiss. Reprinted by permission of
Basic Books, Inc., Publishers.

LIBRARY OF CONGRESS CATALOGING IN PUBLICATION DATA
Myers, Edward.
When parents die.
Bibliography: p.
Includes index.
1. Bereavement—Psychological aspects. 2. Adult
children—Psychology. 3. Parents—Death—Psychological
aspects. I. Title.
BF575.G7M94 1986 155.9'137 85-40790
ISBN 0-670-80771-0

Printed in the United States of America by
R. R. Donnelley & Sons Company, Harrisonburg, Virginia
Set in Trump Mediaeval
Design by Victoria Hartman

In memory of
Francis Milton Myers
1917–1972
and
Estela Montemayor Myers
1913–1981

PREFACE

When Parents Die originates in personal experience. Six years ago, when my mother suffered a series of massive strokes, I found myself dealing with the complex issues of illness and death and grief. "Found myself dealing with"— this phrase just about sums up my situation. I felt as if I had wakened into someone else's life, not my own. The place and the faces were familiar, but everything else had changed literally overnight. Yet there was no alternative to coping with what had happened.

I *did* cope with it, and in retrospect I suppose I coped fairly well. But the fourteen months of Mother's illness—and, for that matter, the eight or ten months afterward—were the most difficult time in my life. My father had died years earlier; his absence not only affected me in its own right but also compounded my current problems. Most of my relatives lived hundreds of miles away and couldn't offer much help. At age thirty, I had few friends who had ever dealt with problems like those facing me. And so the period of my mother's illness and its aftermath was complex both for the practical tasks it presented and for the sense of isolation I felt while dealing with it.

During that time, I often needed information for sorting out options or for making decisions. I also needed support—

not just in dealing with practical situations, but in dealing with their emotional consequences as well. Luckily, some of my friends were generous and patient with me even if they found my circumstances unfamiliar and even threatening. A few were nurses or doctors who could help me locate resources or understand medical issues. Still, it was hit-or-miss. Even locating resources proved more difficult than I would have expected. Making use of them often required more information than I possessed. And, too, the task of weighing alternatives and making decisions was emotionally stressful. The year of my mother's illness was lonely and exhausting. I discovered that many people found my situation more complex and stressful than they could handle. I understood their reaction. The situation was more complex and stressful than *I* could handle, too. Unfortunately, I had no choice in the matter.

In the years since then, as I discovered how many other people face problems similar to mine, I decided to write a guide for coping with the death of a parent. *When Parents Die* is the outcome of this decision. As mentioned earlier, the book has its source in my own family crisis; however, I've based it on considerably more than my personal experience. Interviews, questionnaires, and the borrowed wisdom of experts in the fields of psychology, sociology, and thanatology all enter into what follows.

I should explain what the book is and what it isn't, however, before proceeding. As the subtitle, "A Guide for Adults," indicates, *When Parents Die* can help you find a way through the experience of losing a parent. My hope is that the information provided here will make your task easier and less frustrating than it would be otherwise, and that the variety of situations described will reassure you that your reactions are normal and understandable. In this sense, *When Parents Die* is a self-help manual similar to others written for the bereaved. But the book is *not* a "how-to" manual in the sense of providing a step-by-step answer to the challenges of death and loss and grief. Death is ultimately unknowable. Loss and grief are fundamental aspects of life, yet so complex and subtle that they have defied satisfactory explanation and resolution since the time of Job. I would be irresponsible (not to mention arrogant and foolish) if I claimed that this book could remedy all the pains of bereavement.

Yet the information in this book is worth your time and attention, and it can simplify the tasks before you. By understanding the psychological context of your parent's death, you can also understand how it affects you. By perceiving its consequences on your friends and family, you can also perceive why the event can alter—and sometimes disrupt— even your closest relationships. By learning of specific resources available to you during a parent's illness or after the death, you can ease your burden and the burden of the people around you.

To achieve these goals, *When Parents Die* moves from general to specific issues. Chapter One starts by posing some questions about parental loss, and by considering four people's experiences with it. Chapter Two begins to explore the nature of parental loss by examining loss more generally—that is, the nature of loss following *any* close relative's or friend's death. Chapter Three narrows the focus: if loss of any kind has certain effects, what are the specific consequences of loss following a parent's death? This chapter provides a partial answer. To explore the question further, Chapter Four proceeds to describe the consequences of loss following a parent's sudden death, and Chapter Five considers the consequences following a parent's slow decline.

But in addition to mapping out these issues, *When Parents Die* also provides some specific suggestions for dealing with them. Chapters Six through Eight address a variety of personal and family matters, ranging from funerals and estates to sibling conflicts and personal changes. Chapter

Nine delves into the possibility of counseling or psychotherapy following a parent's death. Finally, Chapter Ten rounds out the book with some personal comments and reflections.

One last matter. Although I've written *When Parents Die* primarily for readers whose parents have already died, I believe that the book may also be useful during a parent's illness. The reason is that your parent's illness (especially a terminal illness) may evoke many of the same fears and worries that arise in the aftermath of the death itself. In addition, Chapter Five offers suggestions for resources and courses of action that can make the long haul less traumatic and exhausting. I realize that reading (or even thinking) about a parent's death before the fact is uncomfortable and painful, and may seem insensitive or morbid. Yet understanding events that will change your life and your family's interactions can help you deal with these complex events. How to face the situation is a matter of personal preference. The information, in any case, is here.

I hope that *When Parents Die* makes a difference for you. Whatever your circumstances, I offer you my encouragement and best wishes.

E.M.

ACKNOWLEDGMENTS

Many people have made this book possible—so many that an acknowledgments section allows only a start in thanking them. But here, at least, is that start.

First, I want to thank my wife, Edith Poor, for her supportiveness and patience throughout the several years of my researching and writing *When Parents Die*; and, too, for the acuity of her psychological and literary insights along the way. Most of all, however, I want to thank Edith for her presence in my life during the family crises that inspired *When Parents Die* in the first place.

Gerald Howard, my editor at Viking Penguin Inc., deserves a special kind of gratitude. In working with me on my book, Gerry has been both trusting and intellectually rigorous. These well-balanced attributes make Gerry the kind of editor that many writers need but few find. I feel lucky and honored to have worked with him.

I also want to thank my friends and relatives for their own numerous, varied contributions to the project. I wish I could mention them all and describe what they made possible; under the circumstances, I must limit myself merely to listing a few for their special efforts: Tamara Eskenazi, Walt and Paige Garnett, Bertha Gilpin, Joanne Greenberg, Eddie Hirsch and Janet Landay, Marvin and Carolyn Jaffe, Mindy

Jaffe, Denis and Susan Langlois, Pat Leebens, Charles and Carole Montemayor, Alex and Maxine Myers, Dan Myers, the Poor clan (especially Geoff Poor and Susan Poor), Bob and Phyllis Schultz, Amy Shapiro, Bernie and Ellen Spilka, Kay Vaughn, John Wright, and Paul Zak.

Another kind of assistance came from the many psychologists, psychiatrists, social workers, nurses, professors, and other social scientists and clinicians who shared their ideas and experiences with me as I wrote *When Parents Die*. Here again I am unable to thank each of them individually. But the following made crucial contributions to the book: Robert Adelstein, M.S.W.; H. H. Bible, M.D.; Rana Binder, M.S.W.; John Bowlby, M.D.; Henry Coppolillo, M.D.; Robert Cowan, M.D.; Jeanne Dennis, M.S.W.; William K. Dixon, Psy.D.; Noreen Dunnigan, M.S.; Wendy Foster-Evans, M.F.E.E.; Louise Fradkin; Robert Fulton, Ph.D.; Evelyn Gladu, M.Ed.; Susan Gurbino, M.S.W.; Jane Heald; Herbert Hendin, M.D.; Lily Ann Hoge, M.S.W.; Mardi Horowitz, M.D.; Carolyn Jaffe, R.N.; Marvin Jaffe, M.D.; Marcia Lattanzi, R.N., M.A.; Mirca Liberti, M.Ed.; Robert Jay Lifton, M.D.; Miriam Moss, Ph.D., Sidney Z. Moss, M.D.; Evelyn Paley, Ph.D.; Colin Murray Parkes, M.D.; Carol Pierskalla, Ph.D.; Anne Rosberger, M.S.W.; Cicely Saunders, M.D.; Phil Thomsen, Psy.D.; and Robert Weiss, Ph.D.

Fully as significant was the help that hundreds of women and men provided through interviews or written comments. This book would not exist without them. To maintain their privacy, I can't list them here. But I will never forget their openness and generosity in sharing their stories with me.

Last, I wish to thank the PEN Writers Fund for its financial assistance during the final months of my writing *When Parents Die*. The Fund's help made the book a much easier task than it would have been otherwise.

E.M.

CONTENTS

WHEN PARENTS DIE

ONE

NEGLECTED GRIEF

In some ways, there is no death that can seem less unfair, less outrageous, than the death of a parent whose children have reached adulthood. The older generation passes away; the new generation comes into its own. No one expects this process to be simple or painless, but perhaps it is tolerable.

Certainly it lacks the sense of injustice that adds so much psychological trauma to other deaths. A child's death strikes everyone as atrocious: all that potential wasted. A parent's death, too, is especially hard when it deprives young children of the companionship and guidance they need. A spouse's death severs a bond that the partners have made and preserved by choice, often over the course of a lifetime. Suicide and murder leave harsh, complex legacies of pain in their aftermath. But an older parent's natural death—surely this is another matter. An elderly mother or father has lived a long life. After illness and suffering, death may be not only acceptable but welcome. Even the death of a middle-aged parent may prove relatively easy to tolerate, since no matter how tragic, it at least seems part of the nature of things. Also, adult sons and daughters have the advantages of experience and maturity to help them deal with their parents' deaths.

All of this may be true yet somehow still end up small

1

consolation. Even when parents attain the biblical ideal of dying "old and full of days," their adult children frequently feel angry, baffled, shaken, exhausted, and everything else that people feel during bereavement. Justice has nothing to do with it—or precious little. Experience and maturity, too, though certainly important, can be frail shelter from the emotions following a parent's death. As a strong, bright, thoughtful woman said after losing both parents, "I felt as if the roof had been ripped away." Of course, she could have said the same thing in the aftermath of any major personal loss. Grief can strip off decades of confidence and competence in a few seconds. But there is another dimension to this kind of vulnerability. Another woman describes her own experience: "My parents died within ten months of each other, and the loss was truly devastating to me. Despite a supportive husband and two great children, I felt orphaned—truly isolated. I had lost the only unconditional love in my life."

Even at thirty, forty, or fifty, the son or daughter of a sixty-, seventy-, or eighty-year-old parent is still that parent's child. The parent-child relationship remains part of human identity throughout adulthood. Why should the death of a parent not leave its mark, and a deep one?

My mother suffered a massive cerebral hemorrhage in June of 1980. Fourteen months later, following three brain surgeries, multiple complications, continuous hospitalization, and eventual placement in a nursing home, she died. I suspect that she welcomed death by then, but I'll never know; she was comatose or semi-comatose during most of her illness. I certainly can't imagine anyone so bright and vibrant wanting to remain in that state of total, permanent disability. All I know is my own reaction to her death: relief, guilt, sadness, exhaustion, bewilderment.

These emotions weren't unfamiliar. Death hurts, and I

knew it. By the time of my mother's death, when I was thirty-one, I had lost my father, a brother, my grandparents, and several friends. Yet the intensity and complexity of what I now felt surprised me. After all, my mother (as almost everyone reminded me) had lived a full life. She and I had had a good relationship; there was little to regret. And the fourteen months of her decline had allowed me a chance to help her and to get myself ready for her death. Then why did her death hurt so much when it finally happened? Simply because death hurts? Somehow that didn't seem like an adequate explanation. Neither did the loss of our friendship. Neither did any other individual reason I could identify.

(Something was different about this experience. The hurt was different from other kinds of hurt. The loss was different from other kinds of loss) Of course, the other losses had hurt, too, but each in its own way) The closest resemblance to what I felt after my mother's death was what followed my father's. He had died nine years earlier, when I was twenty-two. I had found his death as difficult as my mother's, though in different ways. His death had been sudden, hence unexpected and intensely bewildering. But all in all, the two losses produced similar emotions. Was that simply a personal pattern—a consequence of my particular relationships with my parents? Or was it perhaps evidence of a more general pattern? I wasn't sure, but I started to wonder if an adult grieving a parent's death might not face some specific issues and problems, just as persons grieving other deaths—the death of a child, for instance, or the death of a spouse—face other issues and problems.

Soon I started asking other people how they felt about their own parents' deaths. At first, I asked out of a genuine but rather general curiosity. What had happened? How had the loss felt? How long had their grief lasted afterward? Later, when I decided to write this book, I began interviewing people about their experiences in greater detail. During the past two years, I've also explored the subject by means of a widely distributed questionnaire. (See Appendix A for further information on research methods.)

Little by little, I discovered that there are significant patterns to what adults experience following a parent's death.

You're reading this book, likely as not, because one of your parents has recently died. Perhaps even both have died. Or perhaps the deaths occurred some time ago. Or perhaps one or both of your parents are still alive but are terminally ill. One way or another, you're feeling some difficult emotions about what has happened. You want to understand these events and the emotions they create. Given your situation, what does it matter that "there are some significant patterns to what adults experience following a parent's death"?

It matters for at least three reasons.

One is that if you can see the pattern, you can see where you fit into it. This can help you understand what you went through when your parent died—an event that may have been even more complex than it seemed at the time. Similarly, it can help you understand what you are going through now if your parent is still alive but dying. Understanding these events can help you in turn to understand their effects on you.

Another reason why these patterns make a difference is that they can show you that you're not alone. In all probability, you're feeling what most people feel in the aftermath of a parent's death. People's situations vary, of course—the length of a parent's illness, the circumstances of an accident, the ways in which family members help or don't help each other at the time. Emotional responses, too, differ from one person to another. Still, it's safe to say that if you asked a group of men and women to describe their feelings after a parent's death, and if they answered without fear of saying the "wrong" thing, then most of them would describe a mixture of sadness, depression, hurt, anger, bewilderment, and loss similar to what you're feeling now. What you may fear is an "excessive" or "deficient" response to your parent's death is probably normal. You're in good company.

But there's still another reason why these patterns matter: nobody has paid much attention to them. In fact, our entire culture has more or less ignored what adults experience following the death of their parents. Yet five percent of the United States population loses a parent within a given year. Given our current population, that means that 11,650,000 Americans lose a parent annually. Loss of a parent is the single most common form of bereavement in this country. However, the overall attitude within our culture has been one of diminishing, even denying, the importance of people's emotions following parental loss. This attitude may, of course, be part of our American tendency to ignore, diminish, or deny the importance of *all* death and grief. But adults' loss of their parents seems to have been even more thoroughly neglected than other losses.

What people tell you after your parent's death is one sign of this neglect. "He lived a full life," they say, as if that fullness somehow fills your own emptiness. Or else they ask, "How's your mother taking it?"—but ask nothing about how *you* feel. Later, if your grief process lasts longer than friends or relatives find comfortable, they point out, "Of course it's sad, but don't parents usually die before their children do? Isn't that just the nature of things?" These various condolences are all well-intentioned. It's not as if people purposefully neglect your grief for your parent. Rather, they just don't consider it to be significant. The unstated message is that when a parent is middle-aged or elderly, the death is somehow less of a loss than other losses. The message is that grief for a dead parent isn't entirely appropriate.

Consciously or not, you hear these messages. Willingly or

not, you pay attention to them. You may end up believing them. The result is that you probably neglect even your own grief.

My own experience is that despite my closeness with both parents, despite my shock and outrage over how they died, and despite my earlier experiences with grief, I somehow expected that I would "get over them" quicker and easier and less awkwardly than I did. I often berated myself for the intense emotions I felt following their deaths. I worried that this intensity suggested some sort of psychological problem. Later, I realized that the tendency to dismiss my own feelings was part of the same old neglect.

The truth of the matter is that even while in the midst of intense grief, I didn't know much about what was happening. Most people don't. And this is the root of the problem.

Which brings us full circle. What *do* adults feel following the death of their parents? How do they deal with the feelings? What do their situations tell you about your own? And what can you do about what you're feeling now?

Before trying to answer these questions, we should consider four people's experiences.* These experiences will provide a sense of context for later discussions, and, too, a feeling for the range of events and emotions that people encounter.

Sometimes there is the death that comes as no surprise— the death of an elderly parent after long illness—the death that causes sadness, anger, and bewilderment less because it happens than because of how it happens.

---

*To protect the privacy of persons who spoke with me in interviews or who answered the questionnaire, I have changed all names used in this book. I have also changed certain details of people's backgrounds (usually occupation and place of residence). The only exceptions to this rule are the psychiatrists, psychologists, and other professionals whom I quote in later chapters; I refer to all of them by their own names.

Leonore, Sixty-three

Leonore Vaughan lives in Colorado with her husband. Three years ago, Leonore's mother, who lived in Seattle, suffered a stroke. Leonore made several trips to Seattle during her mother's early hospitalization; later, when it became clear that she would need long-term attention, Leonore moved her mother to Colorado. Early hopes of caring for her at home proved to be wishful thinking. Leonore's mother needed a nursing home. This situation itself was a difficult change for everyone involved. "You don't want to consign your parent to the nursing home," Leonore says, "especially as long as she is very aware of her surroundings. And she was. But I didn't have much choice. And I didn't have much knowledge of nursing homes. Of the two here, we chose the wrong one."

What followed was a year-long tragicomedy of errors. The doctor seemed more interested in his vacations than his patients. The nurses resented any suggestions or requests that Leonore made. The aides acted as if looking after Leonore's mother were nothing but a tedious distraction from their coffee breaks. The results of such perfunctory attitudes were disastrous.

"One day I saw that Mother was already starting to have some sort of bedsore," Leonore explains. "The staff didn't even lift her out of bed at all, nor turn her very often. I knew that because the other lady in the room was very aware of what was going on, and she would report to me. I had a spy! But several weeks later, I really got myself into trouble with the staff, because I had stopped off almost every morning on my way to work to make sure that Mother was getting her breakfast. I realized then that they weren't even feeding her. They left the tray in front of her—food unopened, everything out of reach, not even a spoon on the tray. They were making no effort to help her. It was very depressing."

Leonore's mother grew worse over the following months. Even switching from one nursing home to the other made no difference; the other facility in town was not much better. Her attitude had declined along with her health. "When Mother realized that her life was going to be like this—bed change after bed change—that was about the time she told me, 'Get ahold of Aunt Mertie. Tell her to get my funeral ready.'" But Leonore's mother's physical deterioration continued for a long time. She developed extensive bedsores, a bladder infection, and other problems. She grew more and more uncomfortable as the months passed. Leonore felt more and more helpless.

"What I was hoping," Leonore says, "was that I could give her some little bits of enjoyment, small though they might be. My daughter was pregnant, and we would bring her by to see Mother. Mother almost didn't seem to recognize her. She would say, 'Hello, honey.' But it almost didn't seem to mean much to her. I felt that she almost didn't recognize what was happening. I hated that. I wanted her not to be in pain, but I didn't want her to miss things. I wanted her to be with us still. But very soon—when she was looking so bad, and I heard her cry several times when they were irrigating her wound—I didn't care about anything anymore. I started praying then—very much. I just felt, though, that it wasn't going to be much longer. I just didn't want her to suffer.

"I remember a birthday party we held for me at the nursing home. I blew out the candles on the cake and wished that Mother would die.

"The next day, she died in her sleep."

There is also the death that causes difficulty both during the parent's illness and afterward, though the surviving adult son or daughter manages to deal successfully with the consequences.

Mark, Thirty-eight

In April 1980, Mark Cernik learned that his mother had been hospitalized for gallbladder surgery. The operation was not an emergency, but Mark decided to visit her anyway. He flew to Minneapolis from Arizona. Within an hour of reaching the hospital, however, Mark received a phone call from his mother's physician informing him that his mother had developed both pancreas and liver tumors. The doctor had not yet spoken to Mrs. Cernik about her condition. Mark was unsure how to proceed; he decided that the doctor himself should explain the situation to Mrs. Cernik.

Mark recalls the frustrations that followed. "It was about one o'clock in the afternoon. The doctor was late. I was standing there by her bed. And she says, 'What is going *on?*' Well, I've never been able to lie to her. I couldn't say, 'Nothing—blah, blah, blah.' So I said, 'Well, it's really serious.' She said, 'The cancer's back.' She had had cancer eighteen years before—breast cancer—and her doctors had felt she was cured. So I said, 'Yes.' And she said, 'How bad is it?' I said, 'I'd prefer that the doctor come so he can tell you everything on the basis of the CAT-scan, because I haven't seen the CAT-scan.' And she said, *'How bad is it?'* And I said, 'You're dying.' The two of us started crying. Then the doctor showed up."

Mrs. Cernik's health deteriorated with astonishing speed. Mark phoned his brothers and sister, who joined him in Minneapolis; but even by the time the family was reunited, Mrs. Cernik was barely conscious. "She was weakening day by day," Mark says. "We could see a dramatic difference. Her face was sunken. Finally, on Sunday, she lapsed into a coma." Mark and his siblings stayed by her bedside for a week. They took turns catching a little sleep at a cousin's house nearby, but mostly they just waited in the hospital.

The following Saturday, while at his cousin's, Mark received a phone call. His mother was on the verge of dying. He rushed to the hospital. "We were all around the bed. I read some of the Scriptures and held her hand. And at ten-forty, she simply stopped breathing."

Mark felt fairly accepting toward his mother's death. His mother had not suffered greatly, and Mark had shared the final few days with his mother and with his family. Mrs. Cernik's equanimity had also helped Mark to deal with the loss. "I was impressed overall by her tremendous sense of faith and resignation. My father had died almost twenty-two years earlier, and I believe that during those years she had thought about the reality of her own death, particularly because she had had cancer in 1962. So once it had dawned on her what was happening, it was as if something clicked in from before, and she could make some sense of it."

But it remained for Mark to make sense of his own place in these events. He spent a week with his siblings, then flew back to Phoenix. "I was absolutely exhausted and numb when I got home. I think I slept twelve hours a day for seven days. The tiredness was part of my grief. Part of it was that I just couldn't cope with what had happened anymore. I just shut down. I didn't want to talk about it; I didn't want to think about it; I just wanted to sleep. And then after that I was able to begin the process."

For Mark, "the process" was more complex than he had expected. It took about six or seven months to work through the most intense emotions. "I'd say I didn't really work it through until a year later, when I moved to San Francisco. In a new work situation, a new community situation, I began to see that I had a lot more grief-work that I needed to do. So I went into therapy, and that really helped me get through the rest of it. And when I faced my mother's death, I also worked through my father's death, which I had been through twenty-two years earlier. Through the process of re-covering some of those memories and being able to cry about them, that began to free me enough that I was able to finish my grief-work."

In the years since his mother's death, Mark has come to

terms with what happened at the time and earlier. "There have been several times since she died when I've had an overwhelming sense of peace, as if everything is really okay. She and I had sort of come to a new relationship with each other in the last five years before she died. Recalling adulthood experiences—those memories felt good. Those still feel very good. For example, I will find myself laughing at different times when I think of things that she used to do. But I'm laughing with her. Yeah, I still have moments of sadness, but it's mostly very pleasant memories that I have now."

Then, too, there is the double death—both parents dying at once, or else one first and the other soon after—which complicates the practical and emotional tasks for the surviving son or daughter.

Cynthia, Thirty-three

Cynthia Sanderson is intelligent, capable, accomplished. As the assistant program director of an American symphony orchestra, Cynthia has already attained many of her most important professional goals. She is ambitious yet also at peace with herself. Her husband and her friends provide the warmth and the intellectual stimulation she needs; she also receives a lot of emotional support from her family and her in-laws. "I feel very contented with my life right now," she says. "It's going well. For the last couple of years, it's been going really well."

But she has also faced some personal difficulties severe enough to tax her substantial strengths. Eight years ago, Cynthia's father died of a sudden heart attack. That wasn't her first experience with grief, but it was the most intense. At about the same time, Cynthia's mother learned that she had developed stomach cancer. She died a year after the first diagnosis. Cynthia, despite her strength of character, accomplishments, and supportive family, soon felt a kind of confusion so severe that she sometimes questioned her ability to keep functioning.

"It had been an incredible struggle," she explains. "There was comfort derived from knowing how much we did for her and how happy she had been, and how little pain she had been in during the whole run of the illness, given what cancer can be like." But the loss itself was a huge burden. "I was terrified that I truly would not survive without her. Not that I'd really die, but I'd fall apart." Cynthia's fear resulted from an unexpected new perception of herself. Moments after her mother's death, she and her family members had embraced each other. "And I remember when I hugged my sister, the thought going through my head was, 'My God—we're orphans!' On the one hand, that seemed so crazy. I was twenty-six years old, and somehow I shouldn't be an orphan. I was married, and I had a career, and all of that. 'But we don't have any parents!' And I had been terrified the whole year. I thought, it's bad enough to lose one parent, but I can't live in the world without both parents. It just totally changed my standing in the world."

In time, Cynthia came to terms with her new "standing in the world." Time made a difference, but it wasn't sufficient by itself: she also needed her husband's supportiveness, her friends' patience and trust, and her own creativity and stamina before she understood how her life had changed, and why, and with what effects on the future. The outcome was ultimately favorable. Despite this double loss, Cynthia endured it and moved on with the rest of her life.

But with typical candor, Cynthia admits that her feelings have never resolved entirely. "I was incredibly close to my mother. You know, not a day has gone by since my mother died that I haven't thought about her at all times of the day. I think about her all the time. I think about my father a lot, too. But I *acutely* miss my mother—constantly."

And there is also the death that leaves not only months and perhaps years of sorrow, but which can affect decisions and feelings for a whole lifetime.

Marybeth, Sixty-two

Marybeth Jacobs finished her nurse's training just after the Depression. Despite her mother's preference at the time that she help out with the family finances, Marybeth decided to get married. "Having five children and a husband who didn't provide," she says of her mother, "she needed each child to help. She never expressed this, but it was pretty obvious: I could help to lessen the burden. Instead, I got married and *didn't* help."

Her mother died of a heart attack soon after that. Marybeth says, "When I look back on it, this was her way out. She felt so burdened that the only way out was to die." As a result, Marybeth has felt responsible on some level—despite knowing intellectually that she couldn't be responsible—for her mother's death. And this has produced what she herself considers a powerful force influencing her life, including her work as a nurse.

"I was devastated by my mother's death, and I think I handled a lot of it by just putting it out of my mind," she explains. "I don't think I ever really dealt with the grief. Or I did to a point. But the rest I couldn't cope with, so I dismissed it. But I think this is why I'm doing what I'm doing now. Nursing is like a payment back. It's a need—an insatiable need I have—to care for people. And I think down deep, if I would admit it, I would say, 'Mom, I'm helping. I couldn't help *you*, but I can help *somebody*.' And I've only started realizing it. All of my working days as a nurse have always been in a critical care area. Why? It's the need to care. It's the need to give. Now, this could be interpreted as very unhealthy. I don't think it is. It's a legitimate way of saying to my mother, 'I'm sorry, and I'm trying to make it up to you.' "

These descriptions reflect Leonore's, Mark's, Cynthia's, and Marybeth's individual personalities and experiences. Even so, the situations they describe are also characteristic in important ways. For Leonore, what seemed especially difficult was helping her mother through a harsh illness. For Mark, it was the aftermath of his mother's death and, too, its ability to evoke a previous loss. For Cynthia, it was several situations at once: the double loss, the practical problems, the loss of a special relationship. And for Marybeth, it was the sense of guilt. Of course, finding one aspect of a parent's death the most difficult doesn't mean that other aspects are not potentially problematic. Nor are these the only kinds of responses that people have to parental loss. The grief process is one of the most individual of experiences, and the process following a parent's death appears to be even more varied than what follows other deaths.

But the main point is that these four individuals say outright what many people feel but have hesitated to admit: losing a parent can be hard. Very hard. Even for an adult.

And there are some important reasons why.

TWO

THE NATURE OF BEREAVEMENT AND GRIEF

The stories that Leonore, Mark, Cynthia, and Marybeth relate in Chapter One provide a sense of what you may experience following your parent's death. Intense, complex, even contradictory emotions; difficult practical problems; multiple changes in how you perceive yourself and others—these are among the most common consequences of parental loss.

To some extent, of course, these consequences follow any bereavement. All losses resemble each other more than they differ. What matters most is that someone you love has died, and the death affects you. Yet there are differences in kinds of bereavement, too, and in their effects. Your experiences following a parent's death will probably differ from the aftermath of other losses.

Before considering the special attributes of bereavement following a parent's death, however, we will explore the subject more generally.

What Are Bereavement and Grief?

"Bereavement is the reaction to the loss of a close relationship," according to Beverley Raphael, an Australian psychiatrist whose recent book, *The Anatomy of Bereavement*,

15

is one of the best on the subject. Dr. Raphael and other experts believe that this reaction is one that human beings undergo to help them adapt to loss. If two people have a significant relationship and one of the people dies, the survivor usually experiences some form of bereavement. The more significant the relationship, the more likely it is that bereavement will be intense. Bereavement is in some respects the cost of emotional commitment.

Although bereavement is a reaction, what follows it is a *process*. This process involves a variety of emotions—sadness, longing, bewilderment, and so forth—collectively referred to as grief; and the process includes social expressions, generally called mourning. Bereavement, grief, and mourning are potentially confusing concepts. What is most important to remember is that these experiences are all part of a process. When someone you love has died, you need a long time to adjust to the loss. The grief process doesn't happen all at once. It occurs over a period of time—often a longer time than you may find comfortable. It can't be rushed or compressed. But the grief process, though painful in many ways, has its own internal logic; if allowed to proceed, it almost always resolves successfully.

There are two aspects of this situation that we should consider. One is that the bereavement and grief are normal. The other is that bereavement and grief, being part of a process, have phases to their development.

The Normality of Bereavement and Grief

For centuries, some people have tended to regard grief as a kind of illness. Even now you probably hear of someone being "sick with grief," or of a person "dying of grief." There is some truth to these perceptions. As Colin Murray Parkes and Robert S. Weiss (respectively an English psychiatrist and an American sociologist) have noted in their book *Recovery from Bereavement*: "After all, grief is a very painful condition that impairs the ability of the afflicted individual to function effectively in everyday activities. It produces a range of somatic symptoms: heaviness in the limbs, sighing, restless apathy, loss of appetite and weight, sleeplessness and languor, with pangs of acute distress. It is an occasion for sympathetic relatives to gather round and speak in hushed tones just as they do at the bedside of the seriously ill."

At the same time, these perceptions of grief as an illness miss an important dimension to what happens during the grief process. Dr. Parkes and Dr. Weiss go on to state: "Yet there are also grounds for regarding grief as the 'normal' accompaniment of a major loss. . . . We see grief as a normal reaction to overwhelming loss, albeit a reaction in which normal functioning no longer holds." A good comparison might be your body's response to a broken leg. The blow to the bone is clearly harmful. You are in pain. If you ignore the injury or expect it to heal overnight, you may do yourself much worse damage than what you have already suffered. But if you let your body's capacity for self-healing do its work, then you will recover. The broken bone may even end up stronger than it was before breaking.

The grief process is more complicated than the healing of broken bones, of course, and subtler as well. But the basic analogy is appropriate. Bereavement is the human organism's adjustment to major loss. This adjustment, as well as the grief you feel as part of it, is a sign of health—not a sign of its absence. Bereavement and grief are normal.

The Individuality of Bereavement and Grief

The grief process is also highly individual. There is no reason why your experience should necessarily resemble what someone else goes through. After all, your relationship with your parent was unique; when your parent dies, your sense of loss will be unique as well.

"Everybody comes into the situation of bereavement bringing with them a whole history," according to Anne Rosberger, a therapist at the Bereavement and Loss Center in New York City. "It's not as if they just came to this point and it's all entirely new. Every time you have a loss of any kind, other feelings around separation begin to surface. So you are bringing with it a lot of your past experience." The personal background of loss partially accounts for the individuality of grief reactions.

For this reason, you should remember that you don't owe anyone any particular emotion, expression, set of words, or gestures during the course of your grief process. If people around you imply that you seem insufficiently grief-stricken—perhaps you're not crying "enough"—then their reaction has more to do with their own expectations than with your feelings. Likewise if you get the message that you're too emotional, too upset, or too sad. Likewise if anyone suggests that you are too giddy, too spacey, too nostalgic. Wendy Foster-Evans, Bereavement Coordinator at the Hospice of Marin, in California, believes that "people need to go through the grief process at their own pace and in their own way. Some people are very private about grief; others are really expressive. Either way, that's to be honored."

Nobody can decide what your parent's life meant to you; the same holds true for your parent's death.

Bereavement, Grief, and Emotions

The grief process usually includes intense emotions. The particular emotions, their intensity, and their duration vary from one person to another. Likely as not, however, you will experience some sort of grief—some sort of emotional reaction to the death and its consequences. Since these feelings are often surprising—either stronger, weaker, or different from what you might have expected—we should explore the range of possibilities.

Shock

One of the most common emotions right after a loss is shock. This emotion is especially common if the death occurs without warning, but you may feel a sense of shock even if your parent has died after a long illness. No matter how aware you might have been in advance, you're never entirely prepared for the death of someone you love.

Dr. Raphael states that during a state of shock, "The bereaved person feels a sense of unreality, as though . . . it must be happening to someone else. The bereaved may feel distance from the horror and its implications, frozen in time. There is a feeling of being in a dream or a nightmare from which he will awake." You may find it hard to believe that someone could be so fully present at one moment and totally gone the next. The death of someone you love seems a strange, incomprehensible disappearing act.

Cheryl B., who is sixty-one, was twenty-four when her forty-seven-year-old father died. She says, "I was very close to my dad when he died of a heart attack with no previous warnings. It took me a long time to realize that it had really happened."

Susan T. experienced a similar reaction—in her case, partly because her father seemed the stronger of her parents. (She is thirty-three; she was twenty-eight when her father died at sixty-three.) "My father was five years younger than my mother, and had never had previous health problems," Cheryl explains. "Everyone in the family expected my mother would die first, so it was a shock that he was the one to become ill."

Shock is generally an emotion that fades within a few days or weeks. Yet at times it can be remarkably durable. If your parent has died in an accident or from an unexpected stroke or heart attack, you may find it difficult to believe that the death has occurred at all. You may find yourself mistaking a stranger's voice for your parent's, or you may catch sight of someone you imagine to be your parent. These perceptual tricks are disturbing. You may worry that you're hallucinating or even going crazy. However, many people experience these tricks of the mind. They are merely a side effect of shock, and almost always are harmless. Once your mind has had a while to adjust to a sudden and confusing change, the sense of shock and its effects will diminish.

Sadness and Depression

When someone you love has died, you will probably experience sadness, depression, or both. The difference between these two reactions is important but often not recognized in our era. Both reactions are common expressions of bereavement.

John Bowlby, the English psychiatrist whose studies of bereavement and grief form the basis of much research on the subject, states in his book *Loss* that "Sadness is a normal and healthy response to any misfortune. Most, if not all, more intense episodes of sadness are elicited by the loss, or expected loss, either of a loved person or else of family . . ." Sadness during the grief process is essentially an emotional response to the finitude of human life. It is a recognition that something important is over; someone important to you is gone.

Sadness may affect you in general ways, as it affected Alice T., who was thirty-seven when her seventy-five-year-old mother died a year ago: "I feel sad sometimes that she is no longer here." Or else the sadness wells up at a particular time. "On Sunday mornings I always called Mother," says Susan C. (She is fifty-one; her mother died recently at seventy-five.) "Now I feel very sad on Sundays." The sadness that these two women express is predictable, given their close relationships with their mothers.

Yet sometimes sadness comes as a surprise. If your parents were old and sick, you may tend to assume that their deaths will not sadden you when they occur; or if they were hostile or demanding parents, you may imagine that you won't feel sad about the end of the relationships. But sadness is usually part of the grief process anyway.

Dr. Bowlby regards depression as a mood that is "an inevitable accompaniment of any state in which behavior becomes disorganized, as it is likely to do after a loss." Depression is a way in which your mind distances itself from disruptive changes in your life and allows you time to reorganize. Depression, however, often seems less an emotion than an *absence* of emotion. It frequently resembles a kind of fatigue.

Many people become depressed following a major loss. Jenny L., for instance, who is sixty-two, lost both of her parents when she was forty-six. Her parents were elderly; Jenny had had a good, long relationship with them. Yet their deaths not only saddened her but depressed her as well. "I was depressed for months after my parents' deaths," she says. Unfortunately, too many people feel that this reaction is inappropriate. As Jenny puts it, "I never told anyone about this, as I feared they would think it was foolish of a fortyish woman to be so upset at the loss of her eighty-year-old parents." But in fact, Jenny's emotional response to her loss is not at all unusual.

What is most important to remember about both sadness and depression is that not only are they normal, but they almost always diminish with the passage of time. Sadness and depression are part of the complicated adjustment you are making to loss. Although many people feel acutely sad or depressed following a parent's death, few end up being overwhelmed by their emotions. Almost all bereaved daughters and sons find that their sadness and depression let up after a while, and that the pain they feel gradually gives way to more comfortable emotions.

(Lingering depression, however, is a potentially worrisome experience. We will examine it, and what to do about it, in Chapters Eight and Nine.)

Relief

Compared to predictable emotions like shock and sadness, relief often worries—even horrifies—many people following a loss. How can you feel relieved that someone you love has died? Our culture prompts you to feel that relief following someone's death is inappropriate. Yet why shouldn't you feel relieved that your parent's suffering has ended? Shock, sadness, and other emotions complicate a sense of relief, but they don't contradict it.

After an older person's long illness, most relatives feel relieved that the suffering is over. "My parents had been ill for four and five years," according to Ron A., fifty-four. (He was thirty when his mother died at fifty-four; thirty-one when his father died at fifty-eight.) "It was almost a relief when they died." You may end up feeling a similar kind of relief— perhaps relief that you are now spared further effort, emotional upheaval, and family conflict. These are understandable emotions.

Relief sometimes follows a parent's death not just because the illness is over, but also because the parent is now gone. For some sons and daughters, this reaction is a consequence of parent-child conflict. Elizabeth F., who is thirty-five (she was thirty-three when her father died at sixty-eight), had "an emotionally distant relationship" with her father. "He was controlling and disappointed in me," she explains. "When he died, I didn't have to bear his disapproval anymore." For others, relief follows a relationship which the surviving adult child may have valued in some respects and resented in others. Olga T. (forty-eight now, forty-six when her seventy-three-year-old mother died) found that "In some ways, her death freed me to develop my own identity. She was a very powerful person, and I spent my years trying not to be swallowed up. I did this in a passive way which kept me from trying things or using my own creative abilities. I find I am now more open to new things."

There is nothing wrong with a sense of relief under these

circumstances. Although everyone wishes that parent-child relationships could be happy and supportive, reality often falls short of these expectations. Relief following the end of a difficult relationship is certainly appropriate.

Regret and Guilt

Perhaps you feel that you should have done more for your parent; you should have done things differently; you should have said more, said less, said something other than what you ended up saying. After a parent's death, any mistakes and errors of judgment made during the relationship can make you feel that you failed or fell short in looking after your parent. According to Dr. Raphael's *The Anatomy of Bereavement*, "Regret over what has been lost, what cannot be achieved now without the dead person, are . . . common emotions." And, too, "Guilt is frequent: it relates to the imperfection of human relationships."

A good example is Jessie Y.'s situation. Jessie is sixty-one. For many years, she and her mother had a frustrating relationship, full of resentments and conflicts. Jessie's mother died a year ago at the age of seventy-nine. Afterward, Jessie found that she "had a tremendous amount of guilt because I was not with her when she needed me. I also felt guilty for years of misunderstandings and for my often callous disregard for her feelings." Guilt can also follow a less problematic but still unsatisfying relationship. Tillie S., who is fifty-two, lost her seventy-two-year-old mother this past year. "I was left with feelings of guilt," she says, "about not having a close mother-daughter relationship, as some of my friends did."

But even a more satisfying relationship can produce regrets. The demands of caring for a sick parent—especially while the adult son or daughter struggles with conflicting responsibilities—are a potential source for guilt. Few people emerge from the ordeal unscathed. Laura E., forty-four, looked after her mother before she died last year at age eighty. Her mother suffered from scleroderma, a connective-tissue disease, and died a slow, painful death. "I still have some guilt feelings which need to be resolved," Laura says. "I still find myself dwelling on her last few days, and how pathetic she looked."

Julie Walker and Marcia Lattanzi, both bereavement counselors at Boulder County Hospice in Colorado, summarize the situation in this manner: "Guilt is a very prominent emotion in bereavement. It is usually expressed in the desire to have *done more* or to have *said* something to the deceased while he or she was still living. In simple terms, it is a punishment of the self for seemingly not living up to one's expectations of him/herself." Guilt is one of the most common reactions during the grief process.

But it's important to keep these issues in context. First, the *presence* of guilt feelings does not mean that you have *reason* to feel them. Guilt may simply be a side effect of ordinary human fallibility. It seems almost impossible to love your parents and not end up feeling guilty when they endure a harsh illness or a sudden death. You want to make a difference for them, but can't—or at least you can't to the degree that you would have liked. And so the guilt and regret well up. They may be subtle; they may be intense. But they are there.

Second, you should remember that the grief process intensifies most feelings. As a consequence of your grief, you may be recalling missed opportunities and errors of judgment in ways that distort their real importance within your parent-child relationship. This is not to say that shortcomings didn't exist and mistakes didn't occur; however, they may not have been as significant as you imagine.

Anger

Like guilt, anger is common following bereavement—though you may regard anger, like relief, as a "forbidden" emotion. How can you be angry at someone who died? How can you be angry at someone *for* dying? Sadness seems appropriate; anger does not. Yet as Dr. Bowlby and other researchers have noted, many people—if not most—feel some sort of anger in the aftermath of a relative's death: anger for being abandoned, anger for being left with bills to pay or problems to solve, anger for having expended so much effort for an ultimately hopeless cause.

Leona N., sixty-three, had a difficult relationship with her father from childhood on. This relationship worsened over the years as her parents' health deteriorated. When Leona was fifty-nine, her eighty-five-year-old mother died. Interactions with her father became more and more infuriating. According to Leona, "He was very manipulative. He would do things like say, 'All the legal papers you'll need are here [in his desk or safe].' Well, those papers were absolutely no help. He was sending out all those signals to sort of keep me alert to his needs." Leona felt angry at her father long after his death.

You may also feel angry not just at your parents, but at medical or bureaucratic authorities along the way, or simply because your parent's death seems untimely or unjust. For instance, when Marcie D. was twenty-five, her father died at the age of sixty. Marcie, who is now thirty-three, accepts her father's death in some ways, but she still feels angry at how the hospital dealt with his illness. "Hospital personnel were very closed toward us as a family, allowing only very short and few visiting minutes," she says. When her father died, "We were allowed to see the body for only a few minutes before he was whisked away forever." Rubie O., thirty-two, who was twenty-seven when her fifty-six-year-old mother died, was furious about the struggle she undertook against the medical profession. "The blatant dishonesty of her oncologist leaves me angry to this day. My sisters and I had *specifically* met with him to tell him we wanted the truth as her condition worsened."

These are all understandable reactions. Anger may not be

pretty or comfortable, but it often makes sense. Your parent's death has put you under stress; it has demanded your time, attention, patience, or self-denial; and it has ultimately deprived you of someone of great significance in your life. Why shouldn't you be angry? What makes anger difficult is that it's often socially unacceptable to express what you feel toward the people or institutions you hold responsible—doctors, nurses, hospitals, and so forth. Or else the object of your wrath is beyond your reach: fate, God, or simply the nature of things. Perhaps the most difficult situation is anger toward your parent. Feeling angry at someone who has died usually seems awkward, unfair, ungrateful.

Yet in some respects, all these kinds of anger are appropriate. Medical personnel and institutions make mistakes. Fate turns out to be unfair. God declines to perform miracles. Even your parents—the people you counted on for so long— now succumb and die. Anger is a predictable reaction to all these developments. There is no reason to feel embarrassed or frightened by your anger. It is, however, important to express it appropriately. Sometimes a counselor or therapist can be useful in sorting out different kinds of anger and anticipating their effects on your life.

Longing

You may find that you can accept your parent's death a short time after it occurs. However, you may also find that the loss produces intense and sometimes protracted longing for your parent. Like other emotions that surface during the bereavement process, longing can cause you to worry that something is amiss. But also like the other emotions, longing is a normal reaction to loss.

Since adults have many kinds of relationships with their parents, longing can take many forms; but the most common is simply wistfulness for whatever had been good and supportive and enjoyable. Hester W. says, "I missed Mother's presence because she was my best friend." Gwen S. explains that after her mother's death, "I felt so alone—like my 'cheering section' was gone. Nobody else cared about mc and my life quite so much." And Cheryl B. says, "I was very close to my dad and very young when he died of a heart attack. I still miss him."

Perhaps you feel that longing for your parent is inappropriate. As an adult, you are mature and independent. You may therefore feel that longing implies dependence. In fact, you can be a fully functioning adult—one who perhaps sustained your parents more than they sustained you—and still feel a sense of longing after parental loss. Longing isn't necessarily a sign of emotional reliance on the parent. Instead, it seems just as likely to indicate how deep the parent-child bond is, and how long it lasts. It's an acknowledgment of how strong a friendship can grow when parent and adult son or daughter accept each other as equals.

Which of these emotions you feel, when, and to what degree, will depend on many circumstances. Some of these circumstances are a result of bereavement in general—that is, a result of the effects that you would feel following *any* loss. Others are more specific to what follows the loss of a parent. Still others are unique to your own personality.

However, now that we've examined them separately, it's worth noting that these emotions don't usually occur one by one, but rather in combinations. And they often occur in a fairly predictable sequence.

The Phases of the Grief Process

During the past several decades, thanatologists—the social scientists who study death and grief—have identified several phases that people go through during the grief process. These phases make it easier to understand what formerly seemed a shapeless, confusing jumble of experiences.

The most persuasive theory of phases during the grief process is that formulated by Dr. Bowlby. Writing in *Loss*, one of the fundamental books on the subject, Dr. Bowlby states that people go through four phases of grieving after the loss of a close relative. These phases are: (1) numbing; (2) yearning and searching; (3) disorganization and despair; and (4) reorganization. Most people experience all of these phases in one way or another. However, as Dr. Bowlby emphasizes, "Admittedly these phases are not clear-cut, and any one individual may oscillate for a time back and forth between any two of them." This oscillation is an important aspect of bereavement. The grief process rarely proceeds in a smooth, even flow from one experience to another. Instead, it often involves a mixture of emotions—sometimes with considerable uncertainty and ambivalence along the way.

In addition, the nature of your relationship and the circumstances of death make a difference in what you experience during these phases. A sudden loss will affect you differently from a loss that you've anticipated. The loss of a parent will affect you differently from the loss of a spouse, which in turn will affect you differently from the loss of a child, and so forth. (We will examine these various differences in Chapters Three, Four, and Five.) But overall, as Dr. Bowlby explained in a recent interview, "I think this general scheme is applicable toward almost all experiences of bereavement. It is either much intensified in certain situations, or very much modified and attenuated. But this overall pattern applies to all forms of bereavement experiences."

One other important consideration: these emotions are often closely interrelated. They can intensify and even trigger each other. For instance, if your parent died after a long illness, your sadness over the long process of dying can heighten a sense of regret that you couldn't or didn't do more to help. Guilt can augment your anger that doctors and nurses weren't more supportive. Anger can in turn feed both sadness and guilt. The interactions can go on and on. The particular pattern of emotions varies from one person to another, or even within one person from one time to another. Sometimes the interactions are difficult to follow, let alone to understand. The important thing is to be aware that the jumble of emotions is almost inevitable. And, too, it will subside.

If you have heard that grief occurs in a fixed set of "stages," it's worth noting that social scientists have developed theories about the phases of the grief process as a theoretical tool, not as a precise way of determining what any one person should or will feel following a loss. The grief process has a certain order to it, but it progresses through what are actually overlapping, fluid phases. You will cause yourself undue worry if you expect your thoughts and feelings to follow a straightforward course during the grief process.

Duration of the Grief Process

How long do these emotions last? This question is difficult to answer. The duration of intense emotions during the grief process varies enormously, and perhaps more so after a parent's death than after other kinds of loss. As Anne Rosberger of the Bereavement and Loss Center says, "Most people want to know, 'How long am I going to feel this way?' When you're in pain, you want to know that there's an end point. You can tolerate a certain amount of anxiety and pain if you know that at such-and-such time, it'll all be over. I wish we had a crystal ball. But we don't. It really is so individually determined."

The comments of the people I've interviewed, and the written remarks on questionnaires, show an enormous range of response. Some people feel strong emotions for only a few days or weeks. Others remain upset for months, even years. What you experience depends on your own personality, your state of physical and emotional health, your relationship with your parent, the circumstances of the death, your social support system, and other factors. Precisely because the interaction of these variables makes for enormously varied responses, you should keep in mind that there is no single "right" sequence of events. Normal responses range from those in which people feel little or no distress to those in which people feel bereaved for several years.

What you can assume is that the intensity of your grief reaction—whatever your particular emotions—most often lets up gradually. Also, these emotions tend to be recurrent. Even when you expect to feel no more anger, sadness, or regret, the feelings can well up again. Such recurrences, like the slow subsiding of emotions, are also normal. Grief is rarely something that you can have "over and done with" and never feel again. Yet if allowed to run its course, the grief process almost always resolves itself satisfactorily.

Bereavement and Parental Loss

As the preceding discussions have shown, bereavement following parental loss shares many characteristics with other kinds of loss. Shock, anger, sadness, and other emotions characterize grief whenever an important relationship has ended. Acknowledging the reality of death, coming to terms with its consequences, and resuming or rebuilding a normal life are inevitable tasks following bereavement. Consequently, when we examine the nature of bereavement following a parent's death, you should keep these similarities in mind.

Yet there is no such thing as "generic" grief. Each kind of relationship produces a somewhat different form of bereavement: mourning a spouse differs from mourning a child, which differs from mourning a brother or sister, which in turn differs from mourning a friend, and so forth. Parental loss, too, has its own special difficulties. What are they? And how do they affect you?

These are the questions we will explore next.

THREE

CHILDHOOD, PARENTHOOD, AND DEATH

"The loss of parents is one of the great watersheds in life." These words, written by Scottish psychologist E. E. Wilkie, provide one of the best summations of the nature of parental loss. A parent's death tends to be one of the more manageable forms of loss. But bereavement is almost always confusing and painful; bereavement following a parent's death is no exception. In particular, a parent's death (and especially both parents' deaths) can challenge you with certain changes in your roles and in your perceptions of yourself as an adult.

Issues Following a Parent's Death

Several issues make parental loss different from other losses. Let's first consider two general issues: attachment, and the social dimension of loss.

Attachment
When you watch a parent holding a newborn baby, you know that powerful forces are at work. You can sense the baby's need for the parent and the parent's protectiveness toward the baby—almost as if a magnetic field were pulling parent and child together. When you watch that parent in-

teracting with the same child a year later, you know that similar forces are at work, though they have changed: what had been the child's helplessness is now a more complex dependence; what had been the parent's total protectiveness is now a mixture of protectiveness and encouragement to explore.

What you have watched is partly the interaction between the child's attachment to the parent and the parent's bonding to the child. Both attachment and bonding are instinctual behaviors in higher animals, including humans, though human beings' expressions of the instinct depend on cultural and personal factors such as sex roles, personality, and upbringing.

Why is attachment relevant to bereavement following a parent's death? The reason, as Dr. Bowlby told me in an interview, is that "Attachment relationships *persist.* The idea that this [attachment] is a very little matter, and just disappears, is not true. It undergoes a metamorphosis as the other generation gets older, but it doesn't disappear in any conceivable sense."

When I interviewed him, British thanatologist Colin Murray Parkes explained this concept in more detail: "The attachment of the child to the mother is something that's essential to the survival of that child throughout its childhood. On the whole, a baby won't survive unless someone comes along and feeds it and protects it from dangers. There's reason to suppose that the attachment between child and parents is just as much an inborn biological entity as having a left arm or a left leg. This is something you inherit. But as the child grows, its need for attachment becomes less and less. On the whole, what seems to happen is that at a certain stage in maturation, the child's attachment to the parent, and the parent's attachment to the child, begin to dwindle."

Unlike most animals, however, human beings do not simply leave the parents and disappear forever. Human attachment behavior is much more complex. "Humans are characterized by an extraordinarily long period of childhood by comparison to all the other animal species," according to Dr. Parkes. "And certainly as a proportion of their total life span, the human period of dependency on parents is much, much greater. Nonetheless, it does appear that at around about adolescence, there is a rather rapid dwindling of attachment to parents, which perhaps explains the amount of conflict that begins to arise at the time. At the same time, this is perhaps associated with the development of sexual bonds to members of the opposite sex of about the same age group. Before very long, there's a tendency to form a further attachment to somebody else."

But Dr. Parkes notes that the shift in attitudes and behavior is not a total change: "This doesn't mean, however, that there is no residual attachment to the biological parents. I think that although that wanes rather rapidly, it remains as a real thing. And there are very few people who stop caring about what happens to their parents at all."

Two implications follow. One is that as a consequence of attachment feelings, both your parents' presence in your life and their eventual deaths will affect you in ways that the lives and deaths of other persons probably will not. These effects are most pronounced during childhood and adolescence, but they occur even during adulthood.

For example, Janice M. is thirty-five. Her mother recently died of cancer at the age of fifty-seven. Janice is happily married, has two children, and works as a nurse. She was not dependent on her mother in any abnormal way. Yet there was a special bond between them, and Janice felt deep distress following her mother's death. "My mother's death has left a great emptiness in my life," Janice says. "She was a stabilizing and loving part of my life, and I feel at loose ends. There are things only a mother can understand. The comforts I could draw from her are gone, and that fills me with great sadness." The intensity of Janice's longing during bereavement is partly a consequence of having lost her adult-to-adult friendship with her mother, but it's also a consequence of lingering attachment feelings.

The other implication of Dr. Parkes's comments is that how you react to your parent's death will depend partly on how far you have proceeded in your own development. There is abundant evidence that children and adolescents suffer adverse consequences from parental loss. Adults fare better. Parental loss is less traumatic for adults because adults are no longer dependent on their parents for material well-being; in addition, adults are less emotionally dependent as well. But since you don't simply cross a line into adulthood—leaving all your childhood experiences behind once and for all—you take some of the old attachment feelings with you. As a result, even a middle-aged son or daughter can feel strong attachment feelings for a parent. And parental loss can create an intense emotional reaction.

Dr. Raphael summarized these issues when she told me, "The loss [of a parent] is essentially a double one—the loss of a parent who is around and known as an adult, but also the loss of the parent who loved and protected one during childhood." Both halves of that loss—but especially the second half—are powerful because of the old attachment feelings.

The Social Dimension

As Dr. Parkes stated during our interview, "A major factor in determining the outcome of any life-change event— whether it is a loss or a gain—is first, the extent to which a person is unprepared for that change; and second, the magnitude of the change." These factors combine to form what Dr. Parkes calls the social dimension of loss—that is, how loss affects your social situation, and how your social situation in turn affects how you react to loss.

The social dimension of loss partly explains why some deaths cause the survivors more damage than others. Dr.

Parkes states that "There is a world of difference between, say, a wife who loses her husband, on whom she is dependent for providing her with a home and income and a whole host of things; and, on the other hand, the experience of a daughter who has left the parental home and has established a separate life before the parent dies. Perhaps the parent hadn't needed the daughter, and the daughter hadn't needed the parent very much. The widow takes a long time to re-learn how to relate to the world—to discover what it means to be a widow. The daughter hasn't much of a social transition to go through."

For this reason, the conditions of economic or emotional dependency make a difference in what changes the death creates in your life. The changes you're likely to experience following a parent's death are generally less drastic than those following many other losses. As Dr. Raphael states, "With the death of a parent, there are fewer tasks of role readjustment in life, because for the most part [the son or daughter] lacks the intensity of mutual need that exists with a spouse." In addition, the circumstances of the death affect the intensity and length of the emotional consequences. Most of us assume that we will outlive our parents; the shock of a parent's death is therefore potentially less intense than the shock following a child's or a spouse's death.

For instance, Robert V. was forty-seven when his father died at eighty-five; he was fifty-six when his mother died at ninety-two. "My parents were old and therefore death was not unexpected," he says. "Our family was close, so I did miss my parents. But their deaths didn't really affect my life too much, since I was an adult and had my life to live, and had my work." Hugh B., sixty-two (he was forty-two when his father died at eighty-one, fifty-two when his mother died at ninety), had a similar response: "There was not much effect on my life. I was in my forties and fifties, had my own family, and had moved away twenty years before. I had my own life separate from my parents. My life was not changed, harmed, or improved in any significant way." Robert's and Hugh's reactions are common among adults, perhaps especially so among men.

However, the social dimension of bereavement is more complex than it appears at first glance. Parents usually die before their children do, but the timing of a particular mother's or father's death may seem especially premature and disruptive. The death may have practical repercussions. Although most adult sons and daughters live independently of their parents, many others—especially those in their college years—still rely on their parents for financial support. Later, grown children may have more complex practical relationships with their parents. Vern J., forty-seven, had had a long-standing business partnership with his father. The father died at age eighty-four last year. In addition to this partnership, father and son were emotionally close. "My father's death was a loss of friendship, love, business partner, and adviser," Vern says, "and it left an empty feeling."

Besides, the social dimension of bereavement depends not just on outward roles, but also on both your parents' and your own emotional circumstances. Even if you attained full independence long ago, you may still rely on your parents for part of your sense of meaning in the world. Moreover, as Dr. Raphael notes, some adults "still have an intense dependent relationship with their parents."

Attachment and the social dimension of loss largely explain why a parent's death affects you as it does. Your lingering attachment feelings tend to make the death more significant than many other losses would be; your practical and emotional independence from your parents, however, tends to diminish the effects. These two aspects of loss interact in complex ways. And there are other conditions in your life that affect them in turn.

One such condition is your age at the time of your parent's death. Age affects not only your social situation, but also the intensity and complexity of your attachment feelings.

Bereavement at Different Stages of Adulthood

According to Wendy Foster-Evans, Bereavement Coordinator at the Hospice of Marin, in California, "There are lots of variables that play into people's reactions [to loss] at various ages. You're dealing with very different issues in your twenties than you are in your thirties, in your forties, in your fifties."

What are these different issues, and how do they affect how people react to loss?

The Twenties and Thirties

The first two decades of adulthood are a time of moving away from the family; a time of exploring new places, people, and experiences; and often a time of establishing and raising a new family. The twenties and thirties are also a time of consolidating a sense of identity. You have probably accomplished these tasks both by distancing yourself from your parents and by retaining contact with them on a different, diminished level.

Because these issues of separation and independence are emotionally intense, and because the parent-child relationship continues to be powerful in its own right, a parent's death during these decades can be disruptive and bewildering. "There are certain dynamics following the death of a parent that are related to developmental concerns," according to Marcia Lattanzi, Coordinator of Bereavement Services at Boulder County Hospice, in Colorado. "That's true of any loss, but it seems to be acutely true for loss of a parent—and especially if that loss is in the early adult years, when one hasn't completely been able to make the separation from the parent. There is some separation—the initial, tangible separation—but you have not made a psychic separation."

The effects of a parent's death often surprise young adults who are self-sufficient in their careers and relationships. Cynthia Sanderson's reaction isn't uncommon. "That whole process of separation and establishing my own autonomy had certainly not been complete by the time my parents died," she states. "I had thought I was quite independent from my parents. I had always lived in different cities. I'd been financially independent from them ever since college. But when they died, I realized how much I had left incompleted on that score." But sometimes the emotional repercussions are even more intense. Tricia R., now thirty-one, was twenty-nine when her father died at sixty-eight. She says, "I was quite surprised to find that when my father died, I had more of an emotional upheaval than I expected. I had concluded that it would not affect my life a great deal. I was emancipated from them. My father's death triggered emotions I hadn't even begun to tap—suddenly I was no one's 'little girl.' My very roots had been shaken."

A variety of circumstances influence what happens if you lose a parent in your twenties or thirties. A parent's death would be disruptive, for instance, if you have started a family and rely on your parents for guidance and support in dealing with new responsibilities. During our interview, Dr. Bowlby posed the following example: "A young woman is twenty-three; she has just recently married and has one small baby. All of a sudden, her mother is killed in a motor crash at the age of forty-five. That sudden loss would certainly lead to all sorts of reactions. I've deliberately selected a young woman with a family whose mother is lost, because I think that that's a very important relationship—a very great emotional loss in every way. I do believe that especially when a woman has young children, her own mother is a very important figure as a guide and comforter and supporter. So if her mother were suddenly to die, then in fact it would be a great blow." An equivalent sense of loss might result for a young woman whose mother served as a role model for professional activities. And something comparable would hold true for a young man losing a supportive mother or father.

Parental loss often has immediate effects, but it can also have consequences that last far into the future. Marcia Lattanzi described to me the following interaction between loss and future events: "If my mother dies when I'm twenty, then when I get married, I will deeply miss her at the wedding. When I have my first child, I will wish she would be there, and she will be missed again. These types of events are hard because they are constant flashbacks. There is unresolved, unfulfilled potential." Gwen S., for instance, is thirty-six. She lost her sixty-three-year-old mother when she was thirty-one. A year ago, Gwen gave birth to her first child. "A lot of the joy of living that I shared with my mother," she says, "I now share with my husband in watching our daughter grow. I really miss not being able to share that with my mother, though." The same sense of wistfulness can result from your parent's absence as you proceed with your career. You may regret your inability to show your parent what you have accomplished—to share an event that everyone would have celebrated.

Although a parent's death may cause less trauma than the death of a spouse or the death of a child, the consequences at this age are often more intense than they would be if you were older. Speaking of this age group, Robert Fulton, Director of the Center for Death Education, told me that "Their [younger adults'] experience is much closer to what we have taken as typical grief reactions."

The Forties and Fifties

In contrast to the twenties and thirties, the following two decades of adult life are likely to be a time of relative stability in your own life but of increasing uncertainty in the situation you face with your parents. Career and family activities are probably your major concerns during your forties and fifties. You may have no new direct responsibilities for your parents; yet your parents' aging is obvious even if they are healthy. If their health is deteriorating, your parents may already rely on you for physical, emotional, or financial support.

Consequently, the forties and fifties can become a time of complex, even contradictory responsibilities. Your elderly parents may require increasing attention—financial guidance, help running errands, medical care, and other sorts of assistance. Your parents may become totally dependent on you in the aftermath of strokes or other illnesses. The decline of their energies or abilities may prompt you to offer as much help as possible. However, the timing is potentially problematic, since it may occur when you are still raising your own children. So you want to honor a commitment to your parents; at the same time, simultaneous responsibilities to the old *and* the young challenge your stamina, imagination, and patience.

Many families manage to resolve these dilemmas. Both elderly parents and their adult children often work toward compromise. The situation can exert considerable strain on all parties concerned, but eventual adjustments may also allow a further development of parent-child relations. For example, May R. is fifty. When she was forty, her seventy-year-old father died. May then became increasingly responsible for her mother, who was ill with congestive heart failure. Of this experience, May says, "I became the caretaker and managed most of my mother's life for the next six years. I became much closer to my mother during this period. Mother's death was profoundly significant. I had the good fortune to be able to provide good care and to have her die in comfortable surroundings. There was an eventual peacefulness for both of us."

You may, however, experience great hardship under these conditions. You may find yourself resenting your parents' growing dependence on you; your parents may resent your inability to solve the problems that age and illness have created. Misunderstandings may accumulate. Decisions about whether your parents should live in their own homes, in yours, or in a nursing home may become particularly divisive. To some degree, these conflicts are predictable. Dr. Parkes explained during our interview that "As the parent gets older and more dependent on the child, this creates a conflict between the child's wish to be caring and supportive of his elderly parent, and the other competing interests in his life. It's almost the rule that children with elderly parents at some stage or other begin to resent them."

These complex situations can produce many different emotional effects when your parent finally dies. Relief is one of the most common reactions—relief partly for your parent, but also for yourself. When she was fifty, JoAnn H.'s parents died at the ages of seventy-eight and seventy-nine. "My father died four months after my mother," JoAnn says. "I believe he literally died of a broken heart. After his death I felt as if a book had been closed in my life. My parents lived sixty miles away and my family went there a couple days a week for several years. It was nice to stay home and get on with our life. They had had a good life and had both been very ill, and I was glad that they had no more suffering."

Sometimes the hardships are so extreme that the emotional aftermath is almost ecstasy. As Elsie N., fifty-one, summed things up when her ninety-two-year-old mother died: "I'm *free!*" But depending on your circumstances, you may also feel great sadness and longing. "Sometimes I feel I will explode," says Susan C., who is fifty-one. Her mother died a year ago at the age of seventy-five. Since then, she has struggled both with her intense emotions and with a sense that they are inappropriate: "I keep smiling so no one will know the pain I feel." There is no reason that you won't feel both relief *and* sadness. As noted in Chapter Two, there is nothing wrong about any of these responses to a parent's death. Their variety reflects the individual nature of relationships and their strength or weakness during this stage of your life.

The Sixties

Marcia Lattanzi believes that "People in their sixties have the hardest time, perhaps, because they are often feeling old at that moment themselves, with tremendous burdens of care-giving; and feeling like they would like some relief, and being taken care of. I see people in their sixties as having some of the most difficult situations with losing a parent."

If you have raised a family, your children will almost certainly have left home by the time you reach your sixties. Their departure leaves you with fewer conflicts in your commitments toward the older and younger generations. This situation may be an improvement over what you might have faced earlier. Looking after elderly parents may be simpler now than it was during the earlier balancing act. On the other hand, there are new disadvantages. One is simply that as you grow older, the tasks of looking after an elderly parent—especially one with major health problems—may become increasingly difficult. For many people, the effort creates genuine hardships. Leona N., sixty-three, encountered multiple problems in attempting to care for her parents. Both her mother and father lived in a small Arkansas town. Leona lived in Chicago during the years before their deaths. Although she was able to make occasional trips to visit her parents and to look after their affairs, the nature of her work as a college professor made this long-distance arrangement difficult. In addition, Leona had suffered a serious back injury just before her parents died. She was hospitalized at the time of their deaths and was unable even to attend the funerals.

Another potential effect if your parent dies when you are in your sixties is the unavoidable reminder of your own mortality. "If you're sixty-five and your mother is still alive, then you might feel that it's not your turn yet," Marcia Lattanzi stated in our interview. "The older you are, if your parents are still living, then your sense of your own mortality is greater. There is a sense that you are on the edge. A parent's death at such a time can make your own life seem intensely vulnerable. I don't think people who are younger are as conscious of that."

One last consideration: some adult children return to live with a parent—sometimes in the aftermath of widowhood, sometimes for other reasons. More rarely, a son or a daughter will never have left home at all. As Dr. Parkes told me, "One of the commonest situations where a grown child has difficulty following the death of a parent is where an unmarried person has a dependent relationship with that parent, so that at the age of sixty, a man or a woman suddenly loses an eighty- or ninety-year-old parent with whom they have lived all their lives, and for whom they have developed a very strong attachment."

For instance, Lucille K. lived with her mother for decades. When she was sixty, her mother died at the age of ninety-five. The death not only faced Lucille with the loss of her closest relationship, but also with the multiple changes in the outward circumstances of her life. "For the first time I was completely on my own, with no one dependent on me even for company," Lucille says. "I had to remake my life, in new surroundings, completely on my own, at a fairly advanced age. Despite new interests, it was an agony of loss and loneliness for me for a long time."

Most people face far less drastic adjustments. Even so, a parent's death can still create a sense of sadness and longing. Sometimes these feelings are a consequence of what has been left undone for many years. Jessie Y., sixty, whose seventy-nine-year-old mother died recently, says, "My mother's death affected me deeply. I had a tremendous amount of guilt because I was not with her when she needed me. The remorse was almost unbearable." Sometimes the feelings are simply the result of losing a cherished relationship. Margaret A., sixty-five, who was sixty-one and sixty-three when her parents died at eight-five and eighty-nine, found that "My parents' death did not alter my way of life or change it a great deal—just left a space no one else can fill." Either way—and in other ways, too—a parent's death can be an event both accepted and deeply regretted.

The Seventies and Eighties

Although few Americans live into their nineties and beyond, enough do that at least some sons and daughters experience parental loss during their own seventies and eighties. There is little information available regarding how they respond to bereavement, and none from my own research. Their reactions appear to resemble those during the sixties: a mixture of relief, acceptance, depression, and sadness. Some people, having reached a sense of peace about their parents' mortality—and perhaps about their own—seem to find parental loss relatively uneventful. But there is no reason why others wouldn't feel the usual emotions even at seventy or eighty. People whose lives have revolved around a mutually dependent relationship, especially, would experience a deep sense of loss. Your parents' extreme old age does not necessarily make you ready for their deaths.

In cases of the elderly caring for the still more elderly—a more common situation than most people realize—the physical and financial hardships are probably considerable. A parent's death under these circumstances could bring a great sense of relief.

No one decade seems to be the easiest or hardest for parental loss. Each has its own special advantages and burdens. Overall, the twenties and the sixties seem to provide the most consistent hardships—the twenties because of sons' and daughters' lingering dependencies on the parents; the sixties because of the parents' growing dependencies on the sons and daughters. But to understand bereavement, we need to look beyond the issue of age.

Sons and Daughters, Mothers and Fathers

Popular wisdom suggests that sons grieve their parents differently from daughters: sons feel less grief, and daughters feel more. The same assumptions suggest that both sons and daughters feel more grief after the mother's death than after the father's. There appears to be some evidence for these beliefs. Yet there is no question that sons can feel intense grief for their parents—for fathers as well as for mothers. What is the reality of the situation?

As with other aspects of parental loss, there is only limited information available. Social scientists have not yet studied the differences and similarities between adult sons' and daughters' bereavement. However, studies of other losses allow conjecture into what these differences and similarities may be. In addition, the research for this book provides some initial impressions.

Sons' Bereavement

Robert Fulton of the Center for Death Education and Research relates this story about a friend: "He was a funeral director for forty years, and he said that the only time he ever had an emotional reaction during the burial of something like six thousand persons was when he was lowering his father's casket into the grave. This after having buried a mother, an uncle, and a brother. As he was holding that casket and helping to lower it, he thought, 'And now I am the eldest male member of my family.' And with that he fainted next to the grave." Dr. Fulton believes that sons experience a kind of "mortality shock" when their parents die. "I think adult sons are threatened. Their mortality is challenged— by the death of the father, particularly. They're really unnerved."

To some degree, this occurs because the father has been a role model for the son's development as a man. Most sons have looked up to their fathers; even those who no longer do nonetheless probably once considered their fathers to be authority figures of some sort, even if in a negative way. However fallible fathers may be, sons retain at least a little of the awe with which they viewed them as children.

Thus a father's death comes as a shock to most sons. One man phrased his feelings in this manner: "When my father died, he was in his seventies. If anything, he was more dependent on me than I was on him by that age. Neither of us needed each other very much. Nevertheless, the thing that surprised me most about it was my sudden realization that when things went wrong, I couldn't turn to him anymore. Although I'd been an adult and thought of myself as an adult for years, there had always been the feeling that if things went wrong, I could always turn to Dad." The father provides the sense of a barrier or gate between the son and the world—even if the son is fully functioning and in no danger of being overwhelmed by what surrounds him. The father is in some respects even a barrier between the son and death itself. In a recent interview, Robert Jay Lifton, a Yale University psychiatrist, explained that "When one loses a father, especially a father who has been a source of strength—and almost any father is to some degree—one then, as a son, really feels a direct line of responsibility and feels open to the world and its blows, because now one is to some strong extent one's own authority."

However, a mother's death is potentially an even more powerful change in a son's life. Dr. Lifton believes that "The loss of one's mother is perceived more as the loss of someone one has experienced intimate love for—or at least a more immediate love." This bond may, of course, also form between mothers and their daughters. A recent English study suggests that a mother's death may be more traumatic than the father's for adult children of both sexes. But this same study suggests that the effects may be especially intense for sons. Mardi Horowitz, an American psychiatrist, has claimed recently in an *Archives of General Psychiatry* article that both sons and daughters seem to find a mother's death harder to tolerate. The possible explanation is that mothers have generally been the primary care-givers for children, so that mother-child attachments are often stronger than father-child attachments.

What seems to matter most in sons' bereavement, however, is the individual relationships established with the parents during childhood and carried into adulthood. A son may be emotionally closer to his mother than to his father, but he could just as easily be closer to his father. Dr. Lifton explains: "There can be very intimate bonds between fathers and sons, and sometimes alienation between sons and mothers. Many fathers can have what we sometimes call maternal qualities, which are perceived very strongly by a son or a daughter." Yet because sex roles and child-rearing customs remain fairly traditional in this country despite recent changes, Dr. Lifton goes on to say that "Having made those qualifications, I think there is a sense for a man of being more responsible and 'on one's own' after the loss of the father for a man, and of having lost someone more intimate with the loss of the mother. So you have some of the corresponding emotion in either case."

My own research indicates some intriguing patterns in sons' and daughters' bereavement. Although some sons found the death of a parent difficult in the ways that Dr. Lifton and Dr. Horowitz have described, many seemed largely untouched by the experience. Their reactions seem more in keeping with Dr. Fulton's comments to me that when parents are elderly, their deaths are "less disruptive, less emotionally debilitating, and generally less significant for surviving adult children" than are other losses. Among the people who described their experiences in questionnaires, Leonard U.'s comments were unusually blunt but not atypical: "I do not think that I was really much affected by the death of either my father or my mother." (Leonard is fifty-three; he was twenty-five when his father died at fifty-seven, and fifty when his mother died at eighty.) Few daughters described their losses in such an offhand manner. Particularly in their forties and fifties, sons appeared to find their parents' illnesses and deaths more a practical task to finish than an emotional challenge to endure. As we will see shortly, daughters seem more frequently to find their parents' deaths emotionally difficult.

It's important to note, however, that these patterns may be partly a matter of what sons *express*, and not necessarily what they *feel*. Cultural expectations influence how people express their grief. For instance, men often restrain themselves from expressions of sorrow and other "weak" emotions. Women generally feel freer to acknowledge and express what they feel following a parent's death, as in many other situations. As a result, there is a risk of jumping to conclusions about both men's and women's bereavement.

Yet the overall response to my questionnaire suggests that men find parental loss less traumatic than women do. Of 183 respondents total, only 35 were men. There may be several explanations for the low response-rate from males: general disinterest, dislike of describing potentially emotional experiences, and discomfort with the specific situation of parental loss. However, of the 35 male respondents, 18 described feeling little or no grief following their parents' deaths. Another 8 described a moderate degree of grief. Only 9 described feeling intense or long-lasting grief. These figures do not necessarily indicate that sons don't care what happens to their parents, or that they don't love them. But many sons' emotional responses seem more muted and shorter-lived than daughters' reactions. Whether these responses reflect relatively distant parent-child relationships, a fear of feeling grief for a parent, or other factors is still uncertain.

Of course, some sons *do* react strongly to their parents' deaths, and for all the usual reasons. For Rod C., who is twenty-nine (he was twenty-eight when his fifty-eight-year-old father died), the chief issue was the suddenness and untimeliness of his father's death: "I can no longer sleep nights. Life makes no sense anymore. I feel cheated." For Jon L., forty, whose father died two years ago at age seventy-six, the problem wasn't the death so much as the relationship preceding it. "Before I can get over his death," he says, "I believe I will have to first come to peace with the relationship we had while Dad was alive. I will have to get over my anger before I can get over my dad's death." And sometimes the death is simply acceptable but unfortunate, with the emotional consequences that often follow. "I do miss the presence of both of them," says Hugh B., sixty-two, of his parents. (His father died at eighty-one, when Hugh was forty-two; his mother died at ninety, when he was fifty-two.) "But I don't know about 'getting over' their deaths. They were special people to me—friends and companions as well as parents. Their absence continues to be significant to me."

In short, although sons *as a group* react to parental loss somewhat differently from daughters *as a group*, the basic issues that individuals face are the same.

Daughters' Bereavement

One possible explanation for the difference between daughters' and sons' grieving lies in the issue of role-modeling. Both sons and daughters model their behavior after both parents to some extent; for daughters, however, the modeling process focuses on the mother.

This is particularly important because the process seems to teach daughters subtler and more varied ways of dealing with human relationships than what sons acquire. Nancy Chodorow, an American psychiatrist whose article "Family Structure and Feminine Personality" describes how men and women differ in their treatment of relationships, believes that while growing up, "Girls emerge with a stronger basis for experiencing another's needs or feelings as one's own." The implication of Dr. Chodorow's theory is that women often seek greater involvement in their friends' and relatives' lives—including in their parents' lives. Dr. Chodorow's theory partially explains daughters' greater degree and intensity of involvement in their parents' activities from youth through old age. It also helps to explain what appear to be daughters' more intense reactions to their parents' deaths. Dr. Fulton agrees with this theory as it applies to parental loss. "Daughters are far more active in the roles here," he told me. "They're probably more moved emotionally. The effect on other relationships following a parent's death is more emotional for women than it is for men."

Daughters may react more intensely not just to their parents' deaths but also to the illnesses preceding them. Women usually put more time and effort than men do into caring for their parents. By contrast, many men distance themselves from their parents' health problems, or at least take a less active role in the necessary health care. As Dr. Parkes states, "Men seem to be either more ruthless or less caught up in the idea of personal responsibility in looking after the elderly."

This situation has several consequences. One is that a parent's illness often takes a more obvious toll on a daughter's time and attention. If a parent has several children, the daughters will probably end up providing most of the physical and emotional care. The potential for imbalance in this regard can be highly stressful. Jenna O., who is forty, spent several years caring for her sick father before his death at seventy-seven. She did so partly because she wanted to help him and partly because her training as a nurse let her help in ways that her relatives could not. But her brothers took advantage of her skills while simultaneously undervaluing them. "My two brothers quite obviously felt I was there to bring ice chips and give back rubs but not make any 'real' decisions," Jenna says. "I invested a lot of my feelings, emotions, and time, and felt very much 'shat' on. I'm glad I did it, but it has left a hard spot toward other family members."

A daughter who has worked hard to care for the parent will also have a greater reservoir of memories and feelings than would someone who has remained distant from his or her parents. An adult son who has made a similar commitment might well have a comparable reservoir of memories and feelings. But since daughters are more likely than sons to make such efforts, they are also likelier to experience the aftereffects. Needless to say, the effects might be pleasant as well as unpleasant—pride as well as frustration, gratitude as well as resentment. But most people will experience a mixture of emotions.

With a daughter's reactions to her father's death, the situation depends (as it does for sons) on the nature of the personal interactions as well as on the general father-daughter relationship. Anne Rosberger of the Bereavement and Loss Center in New York described to me the effect of these individual differences: "If a father was a daughter's mainstay for her sense of security, and if he was important for her sense of self—the complimentor, the one who gave her a sense of well-being—then that loss is tremendous. But if he was a rather shadowy figure, and if the mother was always there and made her feel good about herself, then the mother's loss would be more important."

Alicia R., forty-one, was thirty when her sixty-eight-year-old father died. She had been close to her father, less than close to her mother. "I felt like the lights went out in my life. My father had been the expressive one of my parents. My mother's distance plus her grief made it difficult for me." Elizabeth F., who is thirty-five, had a nearly opposite reaction when her father died at sixty-eight two years ago:

"My father and I had an emotionally distant relationship, but he was controlling and disappointed in me. When he died I didn't have to bear his disapproval anymore."

The father-daughter relationship usually serves as a foundation for the daughter's later interactions with men in general. As a result, the father's death can create an unexpected sense of rejection—even though the daughter knows her father never *chose* to die. (Sons can feel an equivalent emotion, of course.) Dr. Fulton told me, "If a woman loved her father, then his death is a kind of rejection. It's the severing of all those affectional bonds. It's the loss of the male who helped to define her as an attractive or an appealing human being."

Upon her mother's death, a daughter faces the same issues that face a son, but with some additional issues as well. A daughter loses not only the parent who was probably the more nurturing of the two; she also loses her sex-role model. In addition, many daughters have established close adult-to-adult ties with their mothers, and the end of their friendships are painful. This triple loss may account for why so many daughters find their mothers' deaths especially upsetting. It's not as if daughters are dependent on their mothers in any harmful way. On the contrary, their mother-daughter relationships are often unusually healthy and mutually supportive. But the compounding of losses is problematic.

Sally B.'s words are characteristic of how many women describe their situations. (Sally is thirty-nine; she was twenty-three when her sixty-three-year-old mother died.) "She was a very wise mother, and we were close friends. I felt older and a little fearful [after her death], knowing I was 'grown up' and couldn't call Mamma to share the good times and even a few of the bad. There are just things you can tell your mom that only she would understand."

In closing, we should touch on a final issue that affects both sons and daughters: conflict within a parent-child relationship. Disagreements, old misunderstandings, differences in emotional style, and other problems between you and your parents can affect how you react to their deaths. Although it may appear that the passing of a good relationship would be more painful than the end of a bad one, the opposite seems more likely. The end of a satisfying relationship is regrettable, of course, but ultimately the satisfactions seem to linger. Unfortunately, so do disappointments and resentments. As Marcia Lattanzi stated in our interview, "If we have had brokenness in the relationship with our parent—a parent whom we disliked, or from whom we never got what we needed—then no matter what point in one's lifetime the death happens, it is going to be difficult."

Other Aspects of Bereavement

Age and relationships have the two strongest effects on what you experience following a parent's death. However, some other issues can also make a difference in what you feel.

- How old was your parent?
- Was this parent the first or the second parent to die?
- Did your parent die suddenly?
- If the death was sudden, was it a consequence of suicide or homicide?
- Or did the death follow a long illness?

Your Parent's Age

A relatively young parent's death, like the death of any youthful person, strikes almost everyone as more tragic than an older parent's death. During our interview, Dr. Bowlby stated that "There is an enormous difference between a parent dying at around about fifty, say, and a parent dying 'round about seventy or eighty. One case is a premature death; in the other case, of course, it is not." Your parent's age affects you in at least three ways.

One is the sense of relative injustice. That is, a parent's early death seems outrageous; an older parent's death, though sad, probably seems like less of an affront to the nature of things. Tom S., thirty-five (he was twenty-two when his mother died at forty-six), felt a sense of injustice about his mother's early death. "I was angry about the unfairness that she was being cheated out of twenty years of her own life," he says. "That wasn't fair. Fair for Mom's sake. And it wasn't fair for my sake, either." Compare his reaction to Leonard U.'s. (Leonard is fifty-three; he was fifty when his mother died at age eighty.) "When my mother died, I felt relief," he states. "It was obvious that she had lived a full life and was no longer particularly happy as everyone's grandmother. I am convinced that she herself decided that it was time to die."

The second effect is developmental. If your parent is seventy or eighty, you are probably in your forties, fifties, and sixties; as a result, you will feel less intense attachment feelings than would a twenty- or thirty-year-old son or daughter who survives middle-aged parents. Compare Georgia M.'s and Philip R.'s experiences. Georgia, now fifty-five, was scarcely twenty when her mother died at the age of forty-two. "Mother's death was extremely traumatic," she says. "I still needed her. I was not finished; I still needed *mothering.*" By contrast, Philip, who is seventy-two, was thirty-nine when his father died at seventy-nine, forty-nine when his mother died at eighty-nine: "We had outgrown the governor-governee relationship, and dealt with each other with affection and mutual respect," Philip says. "The change [following the deaths] was a regrouping of physical living conditions and of family activities, and a recognition of loss, but mostly an expansion of other activities."

The third effect is essentially a consequence of practical concerns. An older parent may have required extensive carc—whether medical, financial, or of other kinds—often over a long period of time. The eventual death may affect the survivors with relief more than with sorrow. Rosemary E. is typical of this situation. Three years ago, when Rosemary was fifty-three, her eighty-eight-year-old mother suffered a series of strokes. Each stroke incapacitated Rosemary's mother somewhat more than the previous one. Finally, two years ago, the mother died. Of the death, Rosemary says, "It was the year between the first stroke and the death that caused such emotional scars. The death itself was a relief."

The First Parent's Death and the Second's

In addition, your second experience of losing a parent probably differs from the first. The second is potentially easier in some respects; you have had "practice" with bereavement of this sort. But you may find the experience harder instead. Your second parent's death may strike with special intensity.

Sometimes the second parent's death evokes a childhood loss of the first. "Suppose the adult we're talking about is now forty, and loses a parent who is seventy," Dr. Bowlby says. "But suppose that person lost the other parent when he or she was much, much younger. Having suffered a childhood bereavement after one parent died, the reaction to the loss of the second parent—even though much later—may be much intensified." Though mature, you may actually feel a sense of loss more like what a child would experience on losing a parent. The emotional challenge under these circumstances may be less a matter of dealing with the recent loss than of facing the older, more chaotic feelings of abandonment and vulnerability.

Mark Cernik, quoted at length in Chapter One, experienced intense grief following his mother's death. But some of the most complex emotions he felt actually focused less on that recent loss and more on a long-past event: his father's death. Mark was twelve at the time of the earlier loss. His father had died of a sudden heart attack. The loss had been a severe blow for Mark; yet because of his mother's difficult situation at the time, and because of the family tradition of being "strong" in times of crisis, Mark had squelched his feelings of grief. Following his mother's death, Mark entered therapy to deal with his leftover grief. "Once I got into therapy, I realized that I'd never really worked through my father's death," Mark explains, "because I never really buried him. For twenty years, every time the anniversary of his death would come around, I was practically nonfunctional. And so I began, through the process of recalling memories of my father, to deal with it." In a sense, Mark needed his mother's death to deal with his father's.

In addition, the second parent's death can create unexpected feelings even in people who have suffered no early parental loss. One of the most common is a feeling of orphanhood. Paula T., who is forty-four, was thirty-seven when her mother died at the age of sixty-two. Despite her long-established independence, she felt unexpected emotions following her mother's death: "After my mother's death, I experienced feelings of orphanhood. While I grieved the loss of my father after his death [six years earlier], I had not given up the role of being someone's daughter until after my mother died. Then I felt a real feeling of loneliness and emptiness."

This realization hits hard, yet even people who feel it often consider their reaction inappropriate. How can you be an orphan at fifty-eight or thirty-six or seventy? A sense of orphanhood contradicts your sense of adulthood. But these feelings are a normal response to a major transition in your life. For years, you have carried on a relationship with the people who gave birth to you, who cared for you, who raised you from infancy. Your relationship may have been delightful, frustrating, or somewhere in between, but it was almost certainly charged with the primal emotions we have discussed throughout this chapter. When that relationship ends, there is an inevitable jolt.

"No one knows you like your parents, and no one loves you in such an unqualified way as your parents do," Marcia Lattanzi explained during our interview. "So there's always some longing for those relationships. Now, parents don't always *actually* love you that way. But we tend to believe that they've been *the* sustaining relationship for a lifetime. And now they are no longer there." Wendy Foster-Evans describes the sense of resulting disorientation: "When your parents are alive, you have a sense of knowing you belong somewhere; but once they're dead, you're just kind of out there, even if you now have your own family that you've created yourself." The anxiety that arises from a parent's death is partly a longing for people who cared for us in a special way. As Robert Frost said, "Home is where, when you go there, they have to take you in."

Your parent's death can also force you into a realization about your mortality. It isn't just your parent's death that you grieve, but your own. As Geri N., forty-eight, says about her loss of both parents during the past two years: "Probably the most significant effect [of her parents' deaths] is a growing awareness of my own mortality. I am now the older generation and no longer anyone's daughter." Cynthia Sanderson's perception of her own orphanhood prompted a similar insight about herself. "I think what you realize about parents—even when you lose just one parent, but especially both—is that your parents act as an incredible buffer between you and the world. They are a layer of protection between you and many things. Especially death itself."

Sudden Death

A death you have long expected can turn the world upside-down, but sudden death is especially bewildering. It seems impossible that someone you have known and loved for years—someone you may have seen that same day—is now gone forever. This sense of shock is often part of the bereavement following a parent's death.

Sudden death poses a special challenge. The aftermath of a parent's heart attack, stroke, or accident forces a new reality on you without warning. The reality is stark and cannot be changed: your parent is gone. But your sense of the world doesn't change so fast. Like most people, you probably find it hard to believe that the terrible event has really happened. For a long time afterward, you keep expecting the facts to change. This sense of denial—hope against hope—is a normal part of bereavement. It is most pronounced in the aftermath of sudden death. The first task facing you after a parent's sudden death is therefore one of the hardest—to accept as reality what you want most to believe is a mistake or an illusion.

The situation is still more complex if your parent's death was a suicide or a homicide. Under any circumstances, suicide is one of the most difficult kinds of loss to face. Disbelief, hurt, and anger—all normal emotions following a parent's death—are even more intense than usual under these circumstances. Most survivors of suicide also feel guilty about the death, as if they could somehow have rescued the person who died. Sons and daughters whose parents have been murdered feel most of these emotions, too, though in different combinations and to different degrees.

Because of the special issues involved in sudden deaths, we will discuss them at length in Chapter Four.

Slow Decline

A parent's slow decline spares you at least some of the shock that follows a sudden death; it allows you more time to prepare emotionally for what is happening. There is little question that this additional time—months, years, even decades—can make bereavement easier in many ways. It can allow you not only a more gradual adjustment, but also a chance to strengthen already good relationships, to repair bad ones, to heal old wounds, and to say goodbye.

Yet a slow decline involves its own hardships. Your parents may require time, attention, and money that you may not have to spare. Your parents may suffer from painful and debilitating diseases that cause you as well as them great anguish. They may undergo personality changes that strain your relationships with them. All of these circumstances can be difficult in their own right. In addition, these situations can lead to a potentially awkward role reversal: you become more and more the parent, your parent becomes more and more the child.

As with the issues surrounding sudden death, those surrounding a slow decline are complex enough that we will consider them separately in Chapter Five.

The Unpredictability of Bereavement

The result of all the factors we have discussed—your age, your parent's age, your sex, the nature of your parent-child relationship, and so forth—mean that although bereavement and grief following a parent's death are fundamental human experiences, they are also among the most idiosyncratic. "Bereavement following loss of a parent is less the same than other types of bereavement," Dr. Parkes told me. "There is more variety among people's reactions, ranging from the loss being an unmitigated blessing to the survivor, to it being a devastating blow, with the full range in between." Unlike other kinds of loss—most of which follow relatively consistent patterns—parental loss is highly unpredictable. It can be almost anything.

As a result, you may be especially inclined to question whether your reactions to loss are really what you ought to be feeling. Friends and relatives may offer opinions about what you should *really* feel—well-intentioned but often frustrating perceptions and advice that complicate rather than solve your problems. As it happens, almost *all* adults' reactions to parental loss are healthy and appropriate.

But the basic situation still remains. Your parent has died, or is dying. This is a hard time for you. How should you deal with this situation? How long will the feelings last? And how should you come to terms with them?

Having gained an overview of parental loss and its consequences in this chapter, we should now proceed to explore the two basic situations that adult sons and daughters face when their parents die. The first is a sudden death, which we will examine in Chapter Four. The second is a slow decline, which we will consider in Chapter Five.

FOUR

THE CRISIS
OF SUDDEN DEATH

In late April 1972, after living in San Francisco for a while, I decided to move back to Denver, my hometown. I was twenty-two years old. Certain family traditions and the spirit of the times inspired me to make the move without much planning. I decided simply to show up. On May 3, I flew in, arriving at the Denver airport about three that afternoon.

But when I got home, I found a situation totally different from the cheerful family chaos I had expected. My brother's fiancée, Hilary, was the only person at the house. She said, "I don't know how to tell you this, but your dad is in the hospital. He's in critical condition and isn't expected to make it through the day."

We drove to the hospital, where my mother and my brother Dan were already waiting. My father was in surgery. The doctors were unavailable. Nobody could give me the details of what was happening. There *were* no details. There was only a crisis still taking shape. And then, inexplicably, my father was dead.

I don't recall much of the next few hours or days or weeks, but what I do recall is now a permanent memory. I recall going off by myself after hearing the news. I recall crying loudly in a hospital corridor. I recall going home and finding our house incomprehensibly empty and cold. I recall waking up that night, and most nights for many weeks, and wondering for a few moments what was different; and I recall the inevitable jolt that always followed. I recall sitting in the University of Denver campus chapel and watching six or seven hundred people come to pay my dad their last respects. I recall—and recall despite the intensity of all feelings and all thoughts at that time—the odd sense that none of these events could be happening.

The sense of unreality was strange, even ironic. How was it possible, I wondered, that someone's absence could be so *present?* Nothing seemed more obvious, more emphatic, more overwhelming than my father's absence from our midst. Yet the absence seemed an impossibility. How could someone who had been so thoroughly with us now be gone? How could someone who had been so alive now be dead? How could someone who was so substantial now be nothing?

I found myself waiting, watching, expecting my dad to appear at any moment. Surely there had been some sort of mistake. The wrong person had been hospitalized, medicated, operated on. The intensive care unit must have mixed things up. Someone else's father had ended up at the morgue, the mortuary, the crematorium, the cemetery. My father was somewhere else—perhaps ill; perhaps disoriented or amnesiac; perhaps so alarmed by all the medical commotion that he had escaped, hidden, or gone crazy and fled. Anything was possible. With one exception.

It seemed impossible that he had died. He had been a mere fifty-four years old. He hailed from two long-lived families—Scots and Germans who lasted well into their eighties. Surely his warmth, his curiosity, his stubbornness, his temper, or—if nothing else—then his sense of humor would have warded off something as dull and empty and boring as death. Years earlier, I had nicknamed him Codger, a name that we all found acceptable, even amusing, because he was anything but codgerlike. The man had been tall, strong, healthy, and tireless. He had seemed indestructible. Death was out of the question.

Of course I knew that I was deluding myself. Codger was dead. He was gone. I would never see him again. Yet to my surprise and embarrassment, I kept waiting and watching anyway, turning abruptly when I saw someone of his height or build, glancing about when I heard someone with a similar voice or laugh, and literally shaking with expectation when I caught a whiff of a certain tobacco that Codger had often smoked in his pipe. Sometimes I almost questioned my own sanity.

What I didn't know at the time was that my reactions to Codger's death were not only *not* insane—they were entirely normal. They were actually typical of bereavement following a sudden death.

The Sudden-Death Grand Slam

Shock, bewilderment, and disbelief can occur even following anticipated losses, but sudden death usually intensifies these emotions. "When death occurs with little or no warning, and especially if it occurs in the younger years, then an extra parameter is added," according to Dr. Raphael's *The Anatomy of Bereavement.* "There has been no opportunity for anticipation, for preparation beforehand. The death brings an extra effect of shock over and above the normal."

Denial and Disbelief

Following the death of someone you love, you understandably react with temporary denial or disbelief. It just doesn't seem possible that a person who means so much to you can cease to be part of your life. And so your first reaction is to deny or doubt the death itself.

Dr. Parkes and Dr. Weiss, writing in *Recovery from Bereavement,* regard denial as "a type of distancing produced

by a refusal to acknowledge reality." Disbelief is similar—
though it's less a refusal than an *inability* to acknowledge
what has happened. Either way, these reactions are almost
universal during the early phases of bereavement.

Cynthia Sanderson, who was twenty-five when her father
died, reacted to her father's fatal heart attack with a sense of
disbelief. "I was just stunned," she says. "What does this
mean, that he's dead? I couldn't believe that he was here one
minute and wasn't the next. The last conversation I had
with my father was about cars, which was totally typical.
He was helping me decide what model to get. That was the
last time I saw him. And then the next minute I'm told he
doesn't even exist anymore." Later, once she had a chance to
absorb the news and its implications, Cynthia accepted the
reality of her father's death—first intellectually, then on a
more emotional level. But her disbelief was an understandable, perhaps even necessary, first reaction.

Denial and disbelief are important because they allow
your mind to buy time while adjusting to a harsh and hurt-
ful new reality. You shouldn't *cultivate* denial or disbelief,
but you shouldn't struggle against them, either, during the
early days of bereavement. The sense of unreality will pass.
When you are psychologically ready, you will begin to accept the truth of your loss, and to deal with it at your own
rate.

Reactions to Sudden and Not-Sudden Deaths

Social scientists and clinicians have noted differences in
how survivors react to sudden and not-sudden deaths. For
instance, Dr. Raphael writes in *The Anatomy of Bereavement* that when a family member dies from a protracted illness, relatives "may go through a number of processes with
phases of denial, angry protest, and sad acceptance" before
the death has even occurred. These processes can provide a
kind of "head start" in bereavement. By comparison, a family member's sudden death deprives relatives of a chance to

anticipate the death; hence they lack a chance to grieve in advance.

Yet as Dr. Raphael and other thanatologists have noted, the differences between the two situations are more than just the potential for a head start. Dr. Parkes and Dr. Weiss, writing in *Recovery from Bereavement,* a study of widows and widowers, found that expected and unexpected losses often took different courses. "Individuals informed of the unexpected death of a husband or wife did not disbelieve what they were told," the authors state, "but were unable to grasp its full implications. They seemed to be warding off unbearable mental pain. As they came to accept the reality of their loss, they entered into intense, deep grief." In contrast, "The person who was warned of a coming bereavement responded differently. There was, indeed, a sharp increase in anxiety and tension on being told of the seriousness of the spouse's condition and some attempt to avoid accepting the facts of the situation. This anticipatory reaction was not nearly as severe as the reaction of the unexpectedly bereaved. Nor, as described to us, did the reaction appear to be one of grief with its attendant sense of loss and utter desolation." In short, the nature of bereavement itself seemed to differ in expected and unexpected losses.

Is the situation for widows and widowers comparable to what you face following a parent's death? There are, of course, important differences here: the kind of relationship involved, the relative predictability of parents' deaths compared to spouses', and so forth. But all in all, as noted in Chapter Two, the similarities between kinds of loss appear to be more significant than the differences. Among the most notable differences, whether a death is sudden or not sudden seems to be one of the most important considerations in determining how you respond to loss.

Bereavement following a parent's sudden death is, in short, a different experience from what follows an expected death. And in some respects, bereavement following a sudden death is the more potentially problematic of the two experiences.

Abrupt Changes in Circumstances

In the aftermath of almost any close relative's death, you will face changes in your personal circumstances; in the aftermath of a sudden death, you will face these changes all at once. The nature of these changes is similar following a sudden death and following anticipated deaths. However, sudden death can make the changes more difficult.

For instance, you may have to take on new responsibilities in the aftermath of your parent's death. The situation I faced when my father died is a good example. Within a few days or weeks of his death, I needed to perform totally unfamiliar tasks: arranging a funeral, collecting insurance money, investing the funds in stocks and bonds, and deciding whether to sell or keep the family house. Fortunately, my mother was able to do some of these legal and financial chores. I did most of the others. There was nothing that we couldn't keep fairly well under control. The situation was ultimately within our grasp to solve. But the suddenness of having to deal with them was a problem—more of a problem than the tasks themselves.

How should you deal with your own situation? The great variety of individual circumstances makes it difficult to recommend specific courses of action. However, Chapters Six through Nine of this book offer a variety of suggestions that may prove helpful. See Chapter Six, especially, for a list of necessary actions to take immediately following a parent's death. This list applies to parents' deaths in general, not just to those that happen suddenly. But in the aftermath of a sudden death, it's all too easy to forget these important steps.

Denial and disbelief, reactions to sudden and not-sudden deaths, and abrupt changes in personal circumstances all affect you in the aftermath of a sudden death. Before we look at the effects in detail, however, let's explore what is probably the most important factor of all.

Kinds of Sudden Death

In addition to the circumstances we've discussed, there is the question of what *kind* of death your parent died. Whether the situation involved acute illness, an accident, suicide, or homicide makes a great difference in how you face the aftermath, and how you should deal with it.

Acute Illness

The most common cause of sudden death in adults is acute illness. Heart attacks and strokes kill many thousands of men and women each year, often with no warning whatever. In addition, other ailments kill thousands more with only a few days' or weeks' warning—a time span that probably helps the survivors deal with the loss to some extent, but not as much as a longer illness can.

"Because there is such an intense battle for life [in acute illnesses]," Dr. Raphael states in *The Anatomy of Bereavement*, "the possibilities of death may be put aside in the fight for survival. Then the suddenness of the death, despite forewarning, still brings great shock, although perhaps not so much as in those deaths that are immediate." In addition, there are medical crises of the sorts no longer considered routinely fatal—pneumonia, bowel obstructions, appendicitis—which sometimes result in death regardless of modern medical interventions. Medical intervention itself may contribute to the circumstances causing death—either through medical negligence, malpractice, or simply human error.

If your parent dies partly as a result of negligence, feelings of anger and resentment can complicate and intensify your grief. The death is more likely to seem totally wasteful and pointless than if it were solely a result of illness. Gretchen

Z.'s experience may appear to be extreme, but in fact it is regrettably common. When Gretchen was forty, her father, sixty-four, suffered a bout of flu. Because Gretchen's father was diabetic, his internist had him hospitalized. One problem soon led to another. "Daddy improved and then suddenly developed pain in his abdomen," Gretchen explains. "His internist could not detect bowel sounds [the absence of which could have indicated intestinal obstruction] and consequently called a surgeon for consultation. This took place on Tuesday. The surgeon did not bother to come check Daddy until Friday evening. They opened my father and found, due to a clot and lack of circulation, that all but approximately two feet of his intestines were gangrenous." A day later, Gretchen's father died. "The surgeon killed my father by not coming when he was initially called. The hospital mortality board reviewed the case and agreed Dad's death could have been prevented by immediate surgery. All of these things made Daddy's death hard to accept."

In an age when medical technology develops faster than our insights into dealing with it, you may have ended up in situations calling for quick decisions with long-lasting consequences. Did you make the right choices? Should you have picked a different doctor? Should you have agreed to surgery or not? Should you have recommended more aggressive treatment, less aggressive treatment, or perhaps no treatment at all? The answers to these questions and others can affect how you react to your parent's death in many circumstances, but perhaps most of all during a sudden medical emergency, when time is short and pressure is intense.

Accidents

Approximately 78,000 Americans die in accidents each year. If your parent dies an accidental death, you may struggle with feelings that the death was meaningless. Some illnesses allow at least a sense of context: Father had a weak heart, Mother's family had a history of strokes, and so forth.

Accidents offer few such explanations—let alone a sense of significance. A drunk driver swerved into oncoming traffic; a construction crew let some materials fall; a wire short-circuited. Afterward, it may be hard to believe that death made sense in any way.

Another potential problem is that you may have been involved in the accident as well, with consequences for your own bereavement. "If others are involved in the accident, the death may become a shared traumatic experience," writes Dr. Raphael. "It may perhaps involve a battle for survival from personal injury or the relief of having survived oneself and yet the guilt that one should feel this way in the face of another's death." Moreover, some accidental deaths may result in legal inquiries that can intensify survivors' feelings of guilt. The emotional side effects may include an intensification of the confusion and guilt that often linger during bereavement.

Under these circumstances, it may be helpful to find a good counselor to help you through the process of bereavement. Chapter Nine and Appendix B of this book contain further suggestions about relevant resources.

Homicide and Suicide

The most difficult forms of sudden death to accept and resolve are homicide and suicide. Both have all the usual difficulties that follow a sudden death plus especially heavy burdens of anger and guilt.

HOMICIDE

In the aftermath of homicide, "The shock of the death is complicated by hate for the killer and preoccupation with judgment and retribution," according to Dr. Raphael. "The violence of these deaths compounds the trauma and shock effects of sudden death . . . and these responses are difficult to resolve."

In addition to the anger toward the murderer, you would

probably feel anger toward other targets under these circumstances. Evelyn Gladu, director of Omega, a bereavement counseling center in the Boston area, works with relatives of homicide victims. "What seems to be a big target of the anger is the whole judicial system," she stated in our interview. "The fumblings and red tape and all the time involved these days make people almost as angry as the actual perpetrator does." Of course, legal proceedings after a homicide may provide the relatives with a needed sense of justice; yet the length and complexity of these proceedings can be harmful in some respects. First, the legal process, even when ultimately successful, can protract the grief process. Second, if the legal system fails to find, try, or punish the killer, your anguish and resentment may intensify still further.

If you are dealing with bereavement following a parent's murder, how can you help yourself through this difficult time? There are two possibilities to consider. One is counseling. The aftermath of murder is one of the most problematic forms of bereavement. You are dealing with more than just issues of human mortality; you are also struggling to understand issues of sanity and insanity, of good and evil. The first set of issues is difficult enough. The second set is more than anyone should tackle alone. You will help yourself greatly by finding a qualified person to serve as a guide— or at least as a traveling companion along the way—as you proceed to make sense of what happened.

The second possibility is to take part in a victim assistance program. Many states have started instituting these programs to help people through the aftermath of a homicide. Depending on the particular community, victim assistance programs provide a variety of resources, among them trained advocates who can answer questions, offer suggestions, and even accompany family members to hearings and trials. Victim assistance programs are a fairly recent development; they are not widespread yet. By all indications, however, they are a promising resource in the aftermath of homicide. It would be worth the effort to determine if one is available in your area.

In addition, a group called the National Organization for Victim Assistance (NOVA) now coordinates some of these resources from a central office in Washington, D.C. NOVA can supply names and addresses of regional groups, in addition to offering information about relevant issues. To contact NOVA, see Appendix B.

SUICIDE

Of all forms of sudden death, suicide is probably the most destructive in its consequences for the survivors. The reason is not simply that parental loss through suicide is more common than loss through homicide (though this is true); suicide also evokes especially powerful feelings of rejection and hurt. Dr. Raphael explains: "The person has chosen to die, to desert those who are bereaved." Suicide is most traumatic for the survivors because of its legacy "of uncertainty, of guilt, of blame, and of hostility."

A parent's suicide involves an added complication. As we discussed in Chapter Three, virtually all adults retain some level of attachment feeling for their parents, regardless of age or level of day-to-day interaction. If your parent dies through suicide, the death violates these feelings. It literally severs the bond. Suicide feels like a rejection under almost all circumstances, and perhaps even more so when it is a parent's or a child's death. Thus bereavement following a parent's suicide involves some special challenges for most survivors.

Delia R.'s experience shows these challenges and their effects. When Delia was twenty-four, her mother killed herself. Delia had moved away from her family several years earlier and lived in New York when she learned of her mother's death. Her first reaction was shock. "I went almost instantly into a state of almost giddy disbelief," she says. "It was completely incomprehensible to me. I did not feel sorrow. I didn't feel really sad. It didn't sink in. It didn't have meaning. 'My mother is dead.' It was so far from whatever I ever thought would occur. It seemed the most absolutely impossible thing that I'd ever heard." Her initial reaction resembles most other people's when hearing of a parent's death; there is nothing about it exclusively characteristic of what follows a suicide.

But later, months after Delia had returned home to Iowa City, she felt persistent emotions that reveal another dimension of the situation. "Going to sleep, I remember, was a particular kind of torture. There was this tightness, this feeling that the world wasn't right, so I couldn't go to sleep. There was this dreadful feeling . . . that it was true. That Mom was really dead. She had killed herself. It just seemed that it was the worst possible thing that could happen in the world."

Gradually, Delia began to struggle with the most painful aspects of her mother's suicide. One of them was the fact that her mother had *chosen* to die. "A suicide is an *act*," Delia says. "I was always responding and reverberating with the consequences of this act. But the *act* made it as if Mother was always kept alive, was always killing herself. And so I was always at the point of saying—in the present tense—'Why are you doing this, Mother?' or 'Why did you do this?' Instead of being able to say, 'She *did* this. It's done. She's dead. She's gone.'"

Another aspect of the struggle was Delia's realization that the suicide was the culmination of her mother's long drive toward self-destruction. In some respects, this put the event in context, thus making it more comprehensible. It was not just an isolated incident. But in other respects, Delia's understanding made the suicide still more difficult to accept. "There had been many attempts. I've been able to count—piecing together things my father remembers—about five or six. When my sisters and I were little girls, we would every now and then be sent away, and—poof!—off we went to some relative. Now we know: Mother was in the hospital."

For several years, Delia worked her way through the details of her mother's death, what preceded it, and what followed. She dealt with all of the emotions that survivors of suicide must face: confusion, anger, guilt. She also dealt with a fear common among survivors of suicide—the fear that she would "inherit" her mother's self-destructiveness. Now, several years later, Delia has come to terms with most of these issues.

But there's no question that the aftermath of a suicide often requires more time and patience and energy than other losses do. Even the time involved struck Delia as greater than she had expected. "I'm actually more *now* like I thought I would have been after she died. I get real weepy. I miss her. I couldn't even think about her, I didn't start missing her, for at least two years, if not longer. I cry much more easily now. There's some sense of loss in my system that I don't even connect necessarily to Mom, but I know that's what it is. Now I feel like I'm getting at stuff about Mom. That feels fine. I mean, it's sad, but I think it does take this long to sink in."

As with the aftermath of homicide, what you face after a parent's suicide is probably not something you should attempt to confront alone. It's not as if you can't work your way through the issues and feelings on your own terms. To some extent, there's no alternative. Just as your loss is something that only you can experience, the loss is something that only you can understand. But working through it on your own terms isn't the same as proceeding alone. You will probably have an easier, less stressful time if you locate a thoughtful and supportive guide.

Luckily, there are now many resources available for survivors of suicide. Some are organizations like Omega that provide a variety of services to the bereaved. Others specialize in helping families deal specifically with issues of suicide. Chapter Nine explores your options for counseling, therapy, and support groups. Appendix B includes listings of suicide information centers.

Aftereffects

Following a parent's sudden death, you may face certain situations that would be less likely to occur, or would be less intense, following a more anticipated death. These situations are side effects of the suddenness itself, and are sometimes confusing or upsetting in their own right.

Frozen Images

Sudden death can create a special burden during the grief process if the last moments you spent with your parent were hostile, angry, gruesome, or sad. Because of unfortunate timing, an otherwise happy or pleasant relationship ends up tainted by the final image of conflict or suffering.

Sometimes this happens because of your parent's circumstances at the time of death. Rod C., who was twenty-eight when his fifty-eight-year-old father died of a heart attack last year, found himself constantly reliving the last scene. "I keep envisioning my father dead in the living-room chair as I found him when I arrived that night." Rod is struggling not only with the suddenness of his father's death but also with the shock of being the person who discovered his body.

At other times, the problem is less the scene of death and more the surrounding circumstances—your relationship with your parent at the time, your last conversation, or your parent's situation at the time. Leon F.'s experience is an unfortunate example of how these circumstances can haunt a bereaved son. (Leon is sixty-three; he was twenty-four when his father died at the age of fifty-two.)

"I'd been close to my father," Leon says, "but I was in med school at the time—junior year. He was in the hospital, and he was becoming progressively more ill. My mother wrote a letter that it might be a good idea for me to come and see him. I think she was somewhat fearful to put the facts down. It was a very bad time for me to come. And I wrote him a letter that I thought about him a lot, but I'd come another time, when it would be a little more favorable to the schedule I had. Then I got a call that he had died, and he had had this letter—this letter that I had sent him—in his hand. And it took me quite a while to resolve *that*. I'm not sure if it's all resolved even at this point."

If Leon's father had lived even a day or two longer, the letter wouldn't have seemed so heavily charged with meaning. But a sudden death tends to make whatever has happened at the time appear more significant than it would have otherwise.

The significance isn't always negative. Patrick O.'s mother died at fifty-one when he was thirty-two. (He is forty-four now.) "It was entirely unexpected—there had been no illness, nothing to indicate that her heart was about to fail. I was stunned, bereft. I had to see her body before I could believe it. The only mitigating factor—one which has continued to ease my mind—is that she died celebrating her birthday, in surroundings which gave her pleasure, accompanied by the two people she loved most in this world: her mother and her husband. She suffered only momentary discomfort and died in my stepfather's arms."

But generally speaking, a parent's sudden death leaves a sense of uncertainty, distaste, or repugnance in its aftermath. Coming to terms with the unknown or shocking circumstances may be one of your hardest tasks during the grief process. However, the truth of the matter is that "final" images are not as final as they seem. Many people experience a lingering of images or memories of what immediately preceded a parent's death; and when they are violent or painful, these images are often especially tenacious. Yet even these images will fade. In time, you will find that the older, happier memories will return. You shouldn't fear that you will remember your parent only at the moment of death.

Unfinished Business

If your parent dies as a result of an extended illness, you will probably have an opportunity to discuss concerns and worries, to resolve old conflicts, and perhaps even to strengthen your whole relationship. If your parent dies suddenly, however, you will lack the opportunity for these sorts of resolution. You may end up feeling that the relationship with your parent ended with a lot of "unfinished business."

Kevin T. is thirty-five. He was twenty-two when his fifty-eight-year-old father died of a sudden heart attack. The summer before his father's death, Kevin had attempted to bridge the emotional gap between them through a conversation about personal and family matters. Kevin's father was unresponsive. Rather than force the issue, Kevin let things stand; he figured that he and his father could deal with them later. But then his father died.

"I was so struck by the *finality* of it all," Kevin says. "And I suppose the finality was a lot because of that summer. I didn't have time to prepare myself for the finality. I didn't have time to think about it before it had happened. And I felt intense frustration and sadness and disappointment that I would never see him again. It was as if a huge door had closed—*bam!*—never to be opened again. It was very hard to accept that."

In Kevin's case, his father's death and its termination of their father-son relationship caused regret and frustration, but perhaps no other consequences. But the suddenness of death sometimes affects other people even more intensely. A good example of how dramatically a parent's sudden death can affect a son or daughter is the story that Marybeth Jacobs tells in Chapter One of this book. Her mother's death was not the only source of anguish; the relationship had been problematic for a long time. But the suddenness of the death ended any chance of resolution and simultaneously magnified the guilt that Marybeth already felt.

The problem of unfinished business is often particularly upsetting because there is no simple solution to it. It would be irresponsible to claim otherwise. What you didn't do for your parent can't be done now. What you didn't tell your parent can't be said now. Coming to terms with death and loss necessarily involve accepting these unfortunate realities. Yet accepting them doesn't mean that you can't come to terms with them. Chapters Six through Nine suggest a variety of ways in which you can approach the issues of unfinished business.

Acceptance and Beyond

When my father died, I struggled with most of the issues typical of bereavement after a sudden death. I didn't face the special problems that follow suicide or homicide, and even at the time I knew how lucky I was to have been spared them. But Codger's death was nonetheless a huge personal crisis. It was the worst loss I had ever suffered—in some ways, the worst loss I could even imagine.

Just a few weeks earlier, while talking with a friend, I had stated that I could never endure my parents' deaths. I had become too close to them; our relationships were too important to me. My father's death, in particular, would have been intolerable. In an era when many fathers and sons could scarcely speak with each other, Codger and I were the best of friends. No single relationship seemed more secure, more sustaining. I couldn't see how I could ever survive its coming to an end.

I was doing just that less than a month later. What had taken place seemed even worse than what I had dreaded.

The sense of loss was so strong I could actually taste it. But contrary to my imaginings, dealing with loss turned out to be both harder and easier than I had expected.

All the usual emotions hit me at one time or another. First came the sense of disbelief. Then disbelief gave way to longing. We had had such a good time together—there was still so much left to share. Soon another emotion overtook me: rage. This rage was mostly the anger that usually follows a relative's death, but it focused on the realization that my father had died as a result of medical negligence. Rage eventually collapsed into depression. And so it went, one feeling after another—not in sequence, but many at once, jumbled and entangled, seemingly endless.

But in fact they *weren't* endless. Or at least their early, chaotic intensity wasn't. These emotions fluctuated and shifted, but they also diminished. What seemed at first to be overwhelming emotions gradually eased and grew more manageable. Admittedly, it took a long time for life to feel normal again. The first year was a time of tremendous upheaval. Yet even a few months after Codger's death, I could see the return of some stability in my family and within myself. The first anniversary was a reassuring milestone: not only had I survived, I was doing well. And the years afterward grew easier and easier.

I would be lying—or at least kidding myself—if I claimed that all the shock, hurt, and outrage subsided to nothing. What I see from my own experience and from others' is that sudden death leaves a peculiarly durable, frustrating legacy. It takes a long time to deal with the aftermath of sudden death. But its power is not absolute. It is not permanent.

Although the images and memories of your parent's death may haunt you for a long time, they will diminish after a while. You will eventually regain a sense of stability and continuity within your life. You will gain a sense of the past and its place in your family. You will develop a new sense of who your parent was, and of what he or she gave you during your time together.

The fact of the matter is that even the most unexpected of deaths can never overwhelm the reality of whatever was good in your relationship with your parent. Most of the people I interviewed for this book—including those whose parents died suddenly—found that they ultimately returned to a gentler, happier recollection of their parents, given enough time. "Enough time" often means a year or two. It's a long wait. Still, your capacities for equilibrium and health are stronger than the stress of loss. Chapters Six through Nine will suggest ways to explore those capacities.

FIVE

THE BURDEN OF
A SLOW DECLINE

My mother's death, unlike my father's, occurred following a long illness. Despite the cerebral hemorrhage that first afflicted her, despite the complications that followed, and despite the side effects of multiple surgeries that also took their toll, Mother survived well over a year before she finally succumbed. The fight she put up was both moving and appalling. I couldn't help but want her to prevail against her illness. Yet each new crisis—further bleeding, a brain abscess, meningitis, kidney damage, cardiac arrhythmias, epilepsy, pneumonia—left her worse off than before. She spent most of her last year drifting in and out of a coma, helpless, paralyzed, unable even to communicate.

The way she died affected me more than the death itself. Unlike my father's death, which happened so suddenly that just accepting the reality of its occurrence was the most difficult challenge confronting me, my mother's death was hard mostly because of the events preceding it. The earlier loss hardly even prepared me for what I now faced. My mother's slow decline was a totally different situation.

The first few weeks following Mother's collapse were the easiest to endure. They were a time of great fear, but also of great hope. Mother survived one crisis after another. Not only survived—she improved. She regained consciousness, she recovered most of her intellectual abilities, she returned to relatively normal functioning. The doctors were astonished. Mother had come so close to dying that her recovery seemed too good to be true.

Unfortunately, it was. Her "recovery" was little more than another stage in her illness. In the aftermath of two craniotomies, she developed an abscess that required a third operation. She improved again for a few days, then worsened dramatically. Brain surgery is always a calculated risk; even when successful, it can damage neurological function. Mother suffered side effects that harmed her ability to maintain normal consciousness. Within a few months after her hemorrhage, she slid into a near-coma from which she never emerged.

And so we settled in for the long haul. Luckily, I managed to find a fairly good nursing home in Denver. Mother received sufficient attention to keep her comfortable, but not so much as to prolong her life cruelly. The facility was well enough maintained that various family friends felt at ease coming to visit there. And although I had resisted the possibility of Mother's ending up in a nursing home, I could ultimately see no alternative. At least the overall situation was fairly stable.

This stability met a need—satisfied a hunger, almost—that I had been feeling with greater and greater intensity. For fully six months, Mother's condition had changed so abruptly and so often that I never knew what to expect or how to react. One day she was dying; the next she was vastly improved. Neurological diseases can progress even more erratically than most. But the frequency and degree of Mother's reversals and remissions astonished all but her most jaded physicians. (One of the doctors had remarked, "Your mom has survived more crises than any dozen of my other patients combined.") While I was appalled in many ways by the eventual outcome, I felt relieved simply to have the flux of events slow down for a while. This respite also gave me something I badly needed: a chance to think through what had happened.

"I'm going to outlive all of you," she had told me once. At the time, I had believed her. The women in her family often lived well into their nineties. My mother, despite various medical complaints and several near-fatal crises, had the look of someone who could reach one hundred.

Less than six months after she had made her prediction, Mother was paralyzed, semicomatose, and dying; yet oddly, her terrible state seemed like further evidence in her favor. She had survived three brain surgeries and more complications than I could remember. Time after time she confounded her doctors' predictions that *this* was the problem that would do her in. Of course I knew she was stubborn: a foregone conclusion about anyone in my family. And strong: she had her own quiet power. But even oblivious and immobile, she hung on to life with a moving, frightening tenacity.

I both admired and despised her for it. How could I not want her to survive—and how could I not marvel at how insistently she did so? How could I not hope that somehow this force of will or love or fear or just simple instinct would take her a step further: not just to preserve her, but to heal her? And how, when she reached out in the few ways possible—an eyebrow raised, a word mouthed—could I not reach back? But beyond my admiration, I felt a weariness, too, a tedium, even a kind of exasperation. This would go on forever. Surely I would still be visiting her when I was thirty-five and she was seventy-one; when I was fifty and she was only eighty-six; when I was sixty-five and she a mere one hundred and one . . .

On July 24, 1981, my mother died in her sleep.

The Glacier's Progress

If your parent dies after a long illness, the loss is similar in some respects to what you would experience following a sudden death. Your parent is dead. The relationship is over. You must now deal with the loss and, in time, get on with life.

However, the protracted death is different in some ways, and the loss is different, because the *process* of death has been different. You and your parent have probably received more warning about the impending death. In some instances, the warning has lasted for years, even decades. And this aspect of the loss changes its impact: it tends to be less of a shock even if the ultimate result is still a personal tragedy. Weeks, months, or years of warning can give you a chance to accept the forthcoming death, to make sense of it, perhaps even to soften the sadness and frustration that will probably follow.

Yet a parent's long illness can cause its own special hardships, too. A long illness lacks the sheer shock effect of a sudden death, but it can nevertheless create tremendous strain. If a sudden death hits like an explosion, knocking you flat, then a slow decline arrives more like a glacier, massive and unstoppable, grinding you down.

Medical Battles and Other Challenges

Some of the most eloquent stories that have emerged from my research involve adult daughters and sons whose parents got caught in medical quandaries. Time after time, people have expressed anguish not just over their parents' initial medical problems but also over high-tech treatments, over seemingly hopeless outcomes, over doctors' eventual inability or unwillingness to guide the family out of the impasse. Many respondents stated outright that they did not dread their parent's *death;* what they dreaded was the parent's protracted suffering at the hands of well-meaning, well-trained, but overly zealous doctors.

Jacqueline E., for instance, was the sole relative making

decisions for her parents. (She is forty; her parents recently died at the ages of seventy-nine and eighty-nine.) "I had to protect them from too much medical intervention," she explains. Her mother entered a nursing home at age seventy-seven, following many years of declining health. Her condition deteriorated further in the nursing home. The staff, however, insisted on treating Jacqueline's mother aggressively. "My mother fell and hit her head two days before she died, and the nursing home wanted to send her to a hospital for sutures and neurological checks. I refused permission. As we neared the end, it became clear that *nothing* should be done except to increase her comfort, and that risks must be taken to allow her independence and dignity."

People willing to make such decisions can face a hard struggle against the medical powers-that-be. The R. family is a good example of what can happen. The five sons and daughters, scattered throughout the United States, converged on their hometown when their mother suffered a stroke. According to Tricia R., who was thirty years old at the time, "We had been advised that there was no reasonable expectation of her recovery. She was breathing on her own and was being fed with IVs. The hospital was saying we had to insert a feeding tube into her stomach so long-term care would be facilitated. During the eighteen-month period [between her father's death and her mother's stroke], Mother had spoken with all of us children about how much she loathed the thought of winding up in a nursing home. The five children came to a unanimous decision to discontinue the IV and let her die." The R.s made their decision only after consulting with several doctors and a professional ethicist. They then gathered in the hospital for what became a long and emotional deathwatch. "After the IV was removed," Tricia says, "it took Mother six days to die. It seemed a long, terribly long time."

When physicians overrule the relatives' objections and

prolong the patient's life anyway, some sons and daughters back their demands with specific actions. Some transfer their relatives from acute-care hospitals to hospices. Others obtain private-duty nurses for their parents. Still others take parents into their own homes, often at considerable sacrifice to their own domestic stability, and care for their parents themselves. In a few situations, the adult sons or daughters have accepted their parents' requests for help in dying and actively hastened death in ways that would have been impossible within a hospital setting.

One remarkable incident occurred when Jack and Marge N. brought Jack's ninety-one-year-old mother home to die. As Marge explained to me, Jack's mother had decided that she was simply tired of living; she wanted to fast until her body gave out. "After much soul-searching, my husband and I honored her desire to stop eating," Marge states. "After forty days of absolutely no food, she died peacefully in her sleep." Other people hesitate to battle with the medical authorities more than this couple did, but it appears that more and more American families are disinclined to let their physicians automatically have the final say in their parents' care. (Betty Rollin's recent book, *Last Wish*, chronicles a daughter's decision to cooperate with her mother's desire for suicide.)

Another front in the medical battle is the nursing home. Despite the popular assumption that a lot of people blithely "put away" their parents in nursing homes, Americans seem to view these institutions with great ambivalence. Without question, some families ultimately go ahead and place parents in nursing homes too easily, too quickly, too comfortably. But many people attempt to find alternatives and lament the circumstances that make a nursing home ultimately necessary for their parents.

Leonore Vaughan, quoted at length in Chapter One, decided to place her mother in a nursing home only when the alternatives seemed more destructive to her family. "It was a month after Mother's stroke that I took her back to Grand Junction," Leonore explains. "I understood then that we had quite a different situation than we thought originally. I was hearing the doctors, nurses, therapists tell me that it was a nursing home for her, but I kept thinking, 'Well, we must put her in a nursing home right now. But eventually I want her in my home.' I know that I shouldn't have entertained the thought, looking back on it. But it was never to be. Oh, that was hard for me: coming to understand that I couldn't have her in my home."

It is worth noting that the problem with nursing homes isn't always that they are deficient. Although many people express shock and anger at the bad conditions their parents face in nursing homes, sometimes high quality is a problem, too. Birgit A.'s father suffered from an organic brain syndrome (probably Alzheimer's disease) for years. Eventually he was so incapacitated that Birgit, her sister, and her mother placed Birgit's father in a nursing home. "I remember having the feeling of distress at times that they were taking such good care of him," Birgit says. "That's a terrible thing to say, but he had been a man of great capacity earlier. And I knew he would have hated to be like that. They were force-feeding him at the nursing home. And I thought: 'He wouldn't want this to be carried out like this.' I'm sure I was torn, but there were times when I thought, 'They're treating him so well, they're just making it drag on and on.'"

In many ways, the resentments toward high-tech medical technology and low-tech nursing homes are not really two contradictory reactions. They are two expressions of the same frustration. Modern medical technology can keep human beings alive longer than ever before, but even the most advanced machines and therapies often fall short of curing people. In thousands of instances each year, families end up caught on the horns of a medical dilemma.

Chaos on the Home Front

Financial, legal, and medical responsibilities during a parent's slow decline are stressful. Dealing with them requires time and energy, and may also demand that you learn new skills and acquire new information—often on short notice. But in addition to their intrinsic difficulties, these responsibilities often produce side effects that take a further toll.

Your parent's aging can affect you even under the best of circumstances. When your parent is ill—and especially when terminally ill—the resulting responsibilities can become a great burden. Luckily, many families manage to distribute the burden; no one person carries it all. Perhaps your other parent carries most of it. Perhaps your siblings contribute their own efforts. Most family members are willing to make concessions for the common good.

But the situation is often more problematic. If one of your parents has already died, then you and your siblings may end up taking up the slack. Yet you or your siblings may not live in your parent's town, and may in fact live hundreds or thousands of miles away. What then? Just the trips back and forth from one place to another may be disruptive. For example, Rachel L. made at least twenty trips between Albuquerque and New York to help care for her dying father over a period of three years. "After a while, I lost count," she says. "I made so many trips I almost forgot where I really lived." Even if your whole family lives in the same city or town, however, your parent's situation may require frequent trips to a hospital, multiple visits to clinics, or any number of other errands.

In the meantime, your own personal responsibilities haven't disappeared. What about your family? What about your work? How is it possible to juggle so many demands on your time, energy, patience, and sense of humor? Often it isn't—at least not to everyone's satisfaction. A sick parent needs a lot of attention, but all the other duties that make up your life don't disappear just because of the medical crises. Shopping, fixing meals, and running your household are all continuing responsibilities even if the new ones demand your attention. As a result, your parent's protracted illness probably exerts tremendous stress on your family life. The fatigue alone can be crippling. Not just physical fatigue—if anything, the emotional fatigue is often worse. "You work and you work, and you care and you care, but tomorrow you're going to start all over again," as Carolyn Jaffe, a staff nurse at the Hospice of Metro Denver, puts it. "You don't see any progress. You don't see any way out. All you *do* see is the decline, and sometimes you almost feel as if you're on the way down, too."

Why the Slow Decline Is So Emotionally Difficult

During your parent's illness, distinctions between "practical" issues and "emotional" ones are often artificial. The tasks you perform and your thoughts and feelings about them tend to blur. For instance, deciding whether your elderly father should live at home or in a nursing home is a practical matter, but the decision obviously carries an enormous emotional weight as well. To simplify our discussion, however, this chapter has attempted to sort the practical from the emotional issues at least superficially. The preceding sections have dealt with relatively practical matters. But what of the emotional dimension of a parent's slow decline?

Role Reversals

One aspect of your parent's protracted illness that may take you by surprise is the reversal of parent-child roles. In many families, a parent's illness pressures the parent into a role of increased dependence while simultaneously pressuring the adult son or daughter into a role of increased responsibility. The changes involved may be minor and easily accommodated. On the other hand, the changes may be substantial and may cause great hardship to all parties concerned.

Changes in roles are not unique to parents and their grown children, of course. Husband-wife and other mate roles may change when one member of a couple falls sick or suffers an accident; brother-sister roles sometimes change under similar circumstances; other family or even friendship roles may change as well. Obviously the parent-child bond isn't the only nurturing relationship, nor the only one that can take unexpected forms.

But there is a dimension present in role changes between parents and adult children that frequently complicates the situation. This dimension, as discussed in Chapter Three, is attachment. Even in adulthood, you probably retain some intense feelings about the parent-child roles you outgrew but still retain to some extent deep within your sense of self. As a result, a role reversal between you and your parents can be confusing and stressful. Several people I've interviewed were forthright in describing their feelings about role reversals. Cynthia Sanderson was especially blunt: "Throughout Mother's illness I was so aware of the reversal of our roles— that while she was sick, she had become increasingly dependent on me, and I couldn't be dependent on her. And I resented this all the time. I'm not supposed to be taking care of her—she's supposed to be taking care of me! Even though I was glad to be doing that for her, and felt total duty to her and desire to do for her, it was the reversal of the natural situation. A child is supposed to be taken care of by her mother, not the other way around. There was nobody to function in the role of parents. I mean, nobody was my mother."

Your parent's physical or mental decline often forces changes in your attitudes as well as in your actions. "It's very difficult for people to switch roles with their parents," according to Carolyn Jaffe of the Hospice of Metro Denver.

"It's a whole different role from taking care of your own kids. To watch your parents decline and become more child-like, more babyish—that's an awful thing to watch. It's very degrading to watch your parents lose their faculties." These emotional issues are potentially as complex as the practical problems that give rise to them.

Naturally, you aren't necessarily the only person involved who feels uncomfortable with this situation. Your parents, too, may find role changes confusing, awkward, even humiliating. They may resent their loss of independence. They may express frustration, anxiety, and anger about their misfortunes by complaining to the person closest at hand—you. As Dr. Parkes told me, "Parents may feel resentful that you'd let them down, even though you didn't think you did. This is an accusation which old people sometimes make to the young out of their own sense of helplessness or fear, or out of their grief over the loss of their bodily functions, and so on. They take it out on the family." Some parents—especially those suffering from strokes, brain tumors, or other organic brain dysfunctions—may perceive you and other family members with suspicion or paranoia. Depending on the circumstances, new roles may create as much strain for your parents as for you.

The "Sandwich Generation"

These role issues produce a situation that many people have termed the "sandwich generation." Adults in their mid-twenties to mid-fifties fall into the age group which is simultaneously raising children and assisting parents. Even with responsibilities toward *only* the younger *or* only the older generation, most people feel sufficiently pressured; responsibilities toward both results in a tight squeeze.

Matt V. was forty-two when his father died of a heart attack. For several years afterward, his mother lived 250 miles away from Matt and his family. "At first, as she was independent and able, it created no problems," Matt explains.

"But as her health deteriorated and she required more care, it became a problem—to the point where we were forced to place her in a nursing home. This relieved many of our concerns about her physical welfare, but she still required care on a regular basis by members of the family. During the time she started to become less able to care for herself, my obligations became greater at home. My wife died, and I had children ages fourteen, nine, and seven to raise. It was difficult to find time to care for all and make a living during this time."

The problem is that many of the obligations involved, although not mutually exclusive, end up competing for time and attention. It isn't just that "there are only so many hours in a day." There is also only so much emotional energy, only so much patience, only so much self-confidence. If you are raising children while caring for a sick parent, you will inevitably feel the squeeze between two separate realms of obligation. If you are also attempting to work full-time, then the weight of these responsibilities will be almost overwhelming. "Sandwich" is too mild a word.

Double-Binds

If your parent is dying, you're probably finding that no matter what you do, no matter how hard you try, and no matter how well you ultimately accomplish your goals, you always feel as if you have offended someone, cheated someone, or hurt someone. You visit your parent at the hospital, as you promised, but forget to take your kids to the gym. Or you spend Sunday afternoon with your family—a time you badly need—but feel as if you're miles away. (In fact, your mind is still back at the hospital.) Something always seems to be bumping other obligations out of the way. It's impossible to do anything without getting in a fix.

This kind of situation is the good old double-bind. You're damned if you do and damned if you don't. In the case of looking after your parent, it's a situation in which no matter what you choose to do, you will probably aggravate, anger, or hurt someone—or you'll at least *feel* as if you did. If you spend time with your sick parent, then you take time away from your kids, who are may already be feeling lost in the shuffle. If you spend a Sunday with your spouse or friends, then you'll disappoint your parent, who wanted another visit. You can't seem to win. Of course, you probably face similar dilemmas all the time. Adulthood often seems a veritable macramé of double-binds. In some ways, the basic issues are nothing new. But they *are* different—at least in their complexity and emotional consequences.

The difference is partly that there are not only practical double-binds during a parent's illness, but ethical and cultural double-binds as well. One such double-bind is the "heroic measures" question. You want to do everything possible for your parents; if they have suffered some sort of medical catastrophe, you want to rally all the medical and technological forces available to help cure them. Or do you? Would you do *anything*? Would you keep your mother alive even if there was no hope that she would ever live a meaningful life? Or would it be more merciful to let her die? No matter what you choose, you will feel frustration, dissatisfaction, even anguish. Unfortunately, there are few resources to help you make these decisions. (There are some, however; we will discuss them later in this chapter.)

As a result, these double-binds often seem like nooses around your neck. It isn't just a matter of disappointing one person or another. Sometimes it seems more like choosing one relationship over another, or like choosing one *person* over another. How can you not visit your dying father? At the same time, your marriage is under stress, so how can you not spend at least part of the weekend with your spouse? The surface issue—a family squabble, perhaps, or a sullen afternoon with an unhappy parent—isn't the real problem. It may be little more than the problem's focal point. What is at stake are the relationships you value most.

What is also at stake, often as not, is your basic self-respect. You feel a sense of duty toward your parents. You feel a different but similarly strong sense of duty toward your spouse and children. You can spend time with your parents, with your own family, and with both together. Somehow you work things out. What's the alternative? But pulling the whole situation together takes a toll. You want to do as much as possible for everyone—parents, spouse, children, relatives, friends, co-workers, the community around you. Even so, maybe *you* end up getting lost in the shuffle.

Everyone and everything seems to be taking up your time and energy and patience and sense of humor until it's hard to tell if anything's left. Where are you, meanwhile? Somewhere in there, hiding under the bed in your own mental attic.

Anxiety and Dread

Double-binds are frustrating even under ordinary circumstances; they are still more so at a time of crisis. But they are especially intense when your parent is dying. Depending on the particular situation, your parent might die right away or a long time from now. The uncertainty of the situation is an added burden. If you knew that your parent would live only six months, you could plan for that duration. If you knew that six years was the probable time span, you could pace yourself accordingly. But lacking a sense of what lies before you—a sprint or a marathon—makes it difficult, even impossible, to guess the most appropriate response to the situation.

Another complication in this regard is that you may experience a special kind of anxiety in these situations. Although mature and capable, you may experience a sense of alarm at the thought of your parent's imminent death. This feeling is often subliminal and fleeting. At times, however, it can be intense. It's a vestige of attachment feelings—a sense of dependence and a fear of abandonment left over from long ago. It's no longer appropriate, since you are now an adult and capable of living your own life. But the feeling turns up now and then, a reminder of how strong the ties are between yourself and the people who raised you. There's nothing gained by pretending that it doesn't exist. Better to acknowledge it as a legacy of the child-parent bond, and go on.

Living Life "On Hold"

One of the commonest feelings that people experience when a parent dies a protracted death is that life is "on hold." If your sick parent has been hospitalized or placed in a nursing home, then visits, consultations with doctors, and related errands have undoubtedly interrupted your normal activities time after time. If you have taken your parent into your home, then most of your previous routines have changed—perhaps drastically. The circumstances differ from one family to another. But even under the most favorable circumstances, a long haul will disrupt most families. The errands, the expenses, and the physical efforts involved are only part of the disruption. There is also the waiting, the uncertainty. Combined, these factors often produce the sensation that life is in limbo.

A sudden death overwhelms you with shock and disbelief, but the *fact* of the death is there; sooner or later you have to deal with it. In contrast, a slow decline leaves you with an ambiguous situation. You feel hope, despair, sadness, elation, fear, bewilderment, and any number of emotions, one after another, sometimes several at once, as your parent's illness progresses. Sometimes it's hard to know *what* to feel. Particularly when a disease has an erratic course—bad days and good days, crises and resolutions—the emotional effects can be dizzying. The ups and downs are wearisome. For many people, the early months of intense feelings give way to a kind of numbness. It's too late for blind optimism but too early for grief.

Most people feel frustrated when dealing with the situations we have discussed—responsibilities, medical issues, role reversals, and so forth—and when dealing with their limbo-like consequences. Unfortunately, many of these situations don't lend themselves to easy solutions. But there are, in fact, a variety of resources that can make your situation less exhausting and troublesome than if you try to deal with it alone.

Resources

If all our discussions thus far give the impression that many people in most circumstances go through hard times during a parent's slow decline, then your impression is correct. This situation is potentially one of the most complex and demanding in all of adulthood. Of course, some people experience relatively minor difficulties—whether because of abundant financial and social resources, a particular kind of personality, good fortune, or a combination of factors. But the fact remains: many people find that their parents' slow declines create an unusually disruptive and stressful period of their lives.

If you find yourself in this situation, what should you do? Sometimes it may seem difficult to believe that you can do anything at all. The circumstances surrounding a parent's slow decline are often so complex and so intricately bound together that they inspire a feeling of mere resignation. It may be especially difficult to take action during a time of physical and emotional fatigue.

However, regardless of the tangle of problems surrounding you, there is a good chance that you can find some assistance. The following section describes a variety of resources that can ease the burden of a parent's slow decline.

"Traditional" Social Services

During a parent's hospitalization, you may be able to work out certain problems with the help of **hospital social workers** and other in-house personnel. The availability of social workers, and the roles they perform, will vary from one institution to another. In most, however, a social worker can help you understand what services the hospital performs or does not perform; in addition, he or she can serve as a liaison between your family and other institutions in your community. A social worker can suggest possible nursing homes and alternatives to them. Social workers also can provide a sympathetic ear for families who feel that no one has time to listen to their concerns.

But social workers are not the only hospital personnel who can help you deal with the difficult issues surrounding a parent's illness. Some hospitals now employ a person to serve as an **ombudsman**—someone whose specific duty is to hear patients' or families' complaints. Although ombudsmen are relatively rare, they are an important resource when medical attention seems inconsistent, inadequate, or negligent. They can resolve conflicts or misunderstandings without the risks and expenses that can result from lawsuits.

Also, an increasing number of hospitals are hiring **ethicists.** These are specialists—often psychologists, clergy, or physicians—who can help patients and their families deal with increasingly complex medical decisions. Their role is *not* to make a decision for you; instead, they can explain potential courses of action, indicate their likely consequences, and put alternatives into perspective. At a time when more and more families face difficult medical choices, ethicists are an important resource.

Even hospitals that do not have people filling these roles as such, however, often employ someone who can serve a similar purpose. Hospital **chaplains** sometimes can provide trained, sympathetic assistance in dealing with medical issues. They are not just present to offer consolation. Chaplains at many hospitals can offer help in dealing with ethical problems.

Outside the hospital setting, families have a variety of resources available. The range has diminished during the past few years as a consequence of federal and state budget-cutting; even so, adult sons and daughters can probably find help in dealing with their parents in many different circumstances. State or local **departments of social services** usually provide different kinds of help from what social service departments do within hospitals, but those in many communities include personnel who can be helpful following a parent's hospitalization. Social workers can provide information about available services and procedures for obtaining them. Others can assist you with specific problems, such as dealing with Medicare or Medicaid claims. Under other circumstances, you may need to contact the **Visiting Nurse Association**, an agency that can arrange nursing care for your parent at home. The VNA is an excellent resource for some families wishing to avoid nursing homes. For other families, **home health aides** can provide some assistance.

As a start in locating these resources, check your telephone directory under state and local government listings—especially under "Department of Public Health," "Department of Social Services," or similar agencies. You can locate the VNA in the white pages under "Visiting Nurse Association."

Hospices

The use of hospice care is not always appropriate, but many adult daughters and sons—not to mention their parents—find it a reassuring and consoling option. The hospice concept is actually old, not new. Hospice care simply means providing comfort and reassurance to the dying in a peaceful setting. Our culture has become so preoccupied with technological innovations in medicine, however, that even this simple idea now seems a radical notion. As recently as ten years ago, only a few hospices existed in the United States. There are now more than eight hundred. Some are facilities—buildings with in-house staffs. Others are services that provide care in the patients' own homes. Either way, hospice nurses strive to alleviate pain and to reassure fears, but they do not pursue all the efforts to "save" a patient who wants only to die in peace.

Hospices are an especially significant development because they offer you at least one alternative to aggressive (and sometimes excessive) medical technology. Although hospice care is not appropriate for all patients—or even for all terminally ill patients—it's ideal for some. Under many circumstances, it can provide both the reassurance of medical attention and the familiarity of your own home and routines. Your community may have a hospice or even several of them. Calling a local hospital is a good first step when investigating hospices; the institution may even sponsor its own program. If not, then you may be able to obtain names of other facilities. Another route would be to call the National Hospice Organization for the address of the nearest hospice. See Appendix B for the NHO's address and phone number.

Recent Innovative Resources

One of the reasons that hospice care is not appropriate for all patients is that it focuses on the terminal stages of illness. What do you do, however, when your parent is ill or debilitated but not yet dying? For a long time, adult sons and daughters in long-haul situations had few resources available to them. Their problems were too various and too drawn out for most social service agencies. Hundreds of thousands of people lacked adequate practical and emotional support. Within the past few years, however, an increasing number of Americans have taken the situation into their own hands. There are now several organizations that respond specifically to the needs of adults dealing with elderly parents.

Such organizations do not address themselves solely to issues of death and grief. Illness, troubled relationships, and the many burdens that sons and daughters share with their parents are all potential concerns for these groups. They attempt to provide emotional support, guidance, information, and referral services to adults who are experiencing difficult times with their elderly parents. For example, **Children of Aging Parents** (CAPS) not only serves as a resource center for a variety of client needs but also reaches health service professionals through workshops and in-service training. "There are resources for the elderly person," according to Louise Fradkin, CAPS president, "but no mechanisms to help the *family* cope with the elderly person's problems. And since the majority of elderly people either live with their family or else live in some arrangement other than nursing homes—since nursing homes take care of only five percent of the elderly population—you have 95 percent of the people facing this problem."

CAPS therefore attempts to provide various kinds of support to adults who take care of their parents or other relatives. Support includes information on national resources (nursing homes, caregiving services, social agencies, medical facilities), community education seminars, workshops, and peer counseling. Louise Fradkin and her CAPS cofounder, Mirca Liberti, regard their primary goal as helping adults to cope with the late stages of their parents' lives; accordingly, CAPS tries to deal with emotional issues— stress, role conflict, bewilderment, anger, and fatigue—that affect people regardless of whether their parents are healthy, declining, dying, or recently deceased. See Appendix B for further information about CAPS.

A similar organization is the **National Support Center for Families of the Aging** (NSCFA), located in Swarthmore,

Pennsylvania. According to Jane Heald, NSCFA's executive director, "Our purpose is to provide help to families and other care-givers in coping with their responsibilities to aging persons, and help to individuals facing their own aging." To fulfill its goals, NSCFA offers seminars about caring for the elderly, publishes a bulletin about relevant issues, and distributes a series of cassette tapes about dealing with aging parents. In addition, NSCFA can sometimes provide information about resources available in other parts of the country. To contact NSCFA, see Appendix B.

Other organizations have arisen to meet more specific needs when adults take care of their parents. For instance, the growing nationwide concern about Alzheimer's disease has inspired a network of groups to help families deal with this highly disruptive illness. Relatives of Alzheimer's patients can obtain information about relevant services and resources from the **Alzheimer's Disease and Related Disorders Association.** Other organizations serve a similar function for patients and families who are attempting to cope with other problems, among them cancer, heart disease, strokes, kidney disease, diabetes, blindness, deafness, and arthritis. (See Appendix B for descriptions and addresses of these organizations.) In addition, many people have established local self-help groups to address these issues. Although there is no way to discuss all these groups in a single book, you can locate them by contacting the **National Self-Help Clearinghouse** for further details. Appendix B contains this organization's address and phone number.

No matter how complex your problems in dealing with an aging or dying parent, you shouldn't feel a need to solve all of them alone. Even if you have to make the ultimate decisions, you needn't make them in isolation. Many other people are coping—either personally or professionally—with the same problems. Some of these people can provide information, suggestions, or a sense of shared and sympathetic experience that will ease the burden you carry.

The Aftermath of a Slow Decline

If your parent dies following a slow decline, you will probably feel less intensely shocked or bewildered than you would after a more sudden loss. You have probably anticipated what will happen, and you may even be ready for it. This is especially likely if your parent is elderly, or if your parent (whether young or old) has been ill for many years. The emotions involved are not necessarily mild or short-lived. However, bereavement following a parent's slow decline is often more straightforward than what follows a sudden death. You are less likely to double back, psychologically speaking, on the event itself, repeatedly questioning whether it has occurred.

One possible explanation for this phenomenon is what thanatologists have called *anticipatory grieving*. Perhaps you think of grief as starting after the event of death: when the person you love actually dies, then you begin to grieve. But many researchers believe that grief can start, progress, and sometimes even finish long before the death occurs. The first word of a diagnosis, the subsequent medical tests and procedures, the changes in appearance and behavior, and the other events during the parent's illness all trigger thoughts and emotions about impending loss. As Dr. Raphael states in *The Anatomy of Bereavement*, "When there is knowledge beforehand that death is probable, or inevitable in the near future, those who are to be affected may grieve to some degree beforehand."

Another aspect of this issue goes a step further. The relative lack of shock following a parent's slow decline isn't simply a matter of your accepting the inevitable death in advance of its occurrence. It also involves what you may have *done* during that time. Many adult sons and daughters have been either directly or indirectly involved in their parents' care. Such involvement is often difficult and upsetting. But it can also provide unexpected satisfactions. This is not to trivialize or romanticize the hardships involved, but rather to suggest that the chance to work with the parents, to help them, to comfort them, to ease their suffering, often becomes a source of reassurance and consolation for everyone.

Marcella O., who is forty-two, took care of both her parents following their strokes a few years ago. "The stresses throughout that year and a half were enormous," she explains. "The depth of the loss was profound. Caring for them was difficult, but at the same time it provided many opportunities to say what I needed to, to share feelings that we had never shared before, to say goodbye." For people like Marcella, the time together can take some of the hurt out of impending loss.

It can also allow both you and your parent a means of combating some of the overly technological practices that dominate modern medicine. At a time when millions of Americans perceive hospitals to be cold institutions with little concern for the human dimensions of health and sickness, the opportunity to participate in a parent's nursing can become a gift, not a burden. As a result, once your parent's death has occurred, you may recall your efforts during the illness not just with regret and sadness but also with pride and gratitude.

Perhaps most important, the slow decline can allow you and your parents a final chance for closeness or reconciliation. Herbert Hendin, a psychiatrist at New York's Metropolitan Hospital, describes how this can come about. "That period [during a parent's illness] can be an opportunity—strange as it may sound—to try to deal with certain issues with the parent." Strong bonds can grow still stronger. Weak relationships can heal. You may be able to overcome longlasting estrangements. Your parent's illness, no matter how tragic, can become a final chance to develop together within your relationship.

Sometimes what happens affects only you and your parent. May R.'s experience was unusually satisfying for both her and her mother, but it is by no means unique. (May is fifty; she was thirty-six when her father died at seventy, forty-four when her mother died at seventy-seven.) May states, "I became much closer to my mother during this period [of her final illness]. She was relatively comfortable. After two months of nonverbal communication—she could not speak—there was an eventual peacefulness when she died. I held her hand and felt her pulse as she died. It was a peaceful, beautiful experience which I felt privileged and lucky to experience."

Sometimes the experience can affect an entire family. Sarah B., who was in her early forties when she took her mother into the home, describes her experience: "My parents both required a great deal of care and attention prior to their deaths. Hence our lives were disrupted, but I do not feel they were harmed. Over this period of time I saw much growth in our family relationships. I saw growth in our children and knew we were modeling for them what they could not be taught by mere words. I believe we all underwent permanent change—a deepening and a real knowledge of what unity can do in a situation, no matter how difficult."

What happens is rarely simple or straightforward. For most people, a parent's slow decline is a time of anguish, confusion, and fatigue. Yet even under difficult circumstances, many sons and daughters value the final months or years of helping their parents despite the difficulties.

My own situation included both a share of the difficulties and a share of the satisfactions. The fourteen months of my mother's illness were the most physically and emotionally demanding period of my life. During that time, I made most of the decisions about Mother's medical treatment, provided some of her nursing care, handled her finances, and communicated with relatives about all these matters. I'm not sure how I did it. My work as a writer gave me some flexibility, at least. Being a bachelor at the time helped in some respects, too—at least I didn't have to juggle so many responsibilities. But I'm still not sure how I managed. The pressures seemed unrelenting: one crisis after another, unfamiliar tasks in unpredictable sequences, hopes and fears and disappointments tangled and mashed together beyond recognition. Somehow I got through those months. When it was over, I was exhausted in more ways than I thought possible. But I had done what I needed to do. Somehow, it was important and good to have done it.

That's where the satisfaction came in. I'm not at all convinced that I did a good job of looking after my mother, or that I always acted selflessly, or that I understood the consequences of my choices; and I certainly don't believe that I made all the right decisions, or that what I did ultimately helped my mother to any degree close to what I would have liked. Yet despite these reservations—and they are pit-of-the-stomach, middle-of-the-night reservations, not just comfortable daylight musings—I feel sure that I made a big difference for Mother during that time. I wasn't the only one who did: some of our relatives and friends did also. But in our clumsy, fallible way, we managed to take the edge off the harshness of her final year. Perhaps—given mortality and the limitations of human love—that's all I should have expected.

I'm not saying that good intentions set everything right. They didn't. My mother died a gruesome death, and no amount of caring for her overcame the gruesomeness, let alone the death. Neither am I saying that filial duty toward her settled all the issues. Although I felt some sort of duty toward her, it complicated things more than it simplified them. All I'm saying is that the fourteen months of my mother's illness were both intensely difficult and intensely meaningful.

Many of the adult sons and daughters I've interviewed seem to feel much the same. Circumstances differ. For many people, a parent's slow decline is simply an event to endure. That's understandable. It's not a reflection on what someone has done or not done. In the midst of confusion and fatigue, meaning is often an unattainable luxury. But for many of the people I've interviewed, the passage of time—a few years' distance from painful events—has ultimately let a sense of meaning emerge.

At the same time, there's no doubt that despite the preparation a parent's slow decline often provides, despite the opportunities for drawing closer during a last illness, and despite the chance to say goodbye, you may end up feeling merely exhausted and depressed when the death finally occurs. After months or years of caring for a parent, just the physical fatigue can be a major problem. Emotional exhaustion is another matter entirely. And what if the side effects of your parent's death include not only physical and emotional consequences but financial and legal problems as well? How do you deal with them?

The remaining chapters of this book will address these and other issues—issues that come up not only after a parent's slow decline, but also after a sudden death.

SIX

FUNERALS, ESTATES, AND LAWSUITS

So far, this book has focused on why your parent's death affects you as it does. Now we will examine the specific consequences of a parent's death. We will also consider what these consequences mean, and what you can do about them.

Some consequences are legal and financial tasks, such as settling an estate. Others are family issues, such as role changes between you and your relatives. Still others are the personal changes that often follow a parent's death. Each of the next three chapters will explore these various matters.

Not all people end up having to deal with these situations, of course. These chapters shouldn't lead you to worry that a new ordeal awaits you at every turn. Perhaps several of these issues will affect you; perhaps only one or two; perhaps none at all. Think of these chapters as a compendium of possible situations that you may face following your parent's death. Read whichever sections are helpful. Ignore the rest.

One other point: the following discussions are *not* intended as "Ten Easy Steps to Better Bereavement." There are no clear-cut, guaranteed steps to overcoming loss. Little about bereavement is simple. It would be a mistake to reduce one of life's most complex and personal experiences to a series of tips. But these discussions can help to put your own bereavement into perspective, and to provide some resources for dealing with it.

First, the nitty-gritty. Let's start with the practical matters that can affect you following your parent's death.

Funerals and Other Rituals

Nobody finds funerals easy. Yet according to Dr. Raphael's *The Anatomy of Bereavement,* "Many bereaved people find this is a turning point where the full reality of the death hits directly home." The reality of death is painful, but accepting it is a crucial first step in the grief process. Your parent's funeral can help you come to terms with the death in important ways.

"There was some sense of resolution to it," Mark Cernik, whom we met in Chapter One, says of his mother's funeral. "It was a beautiful experience of our own faith, of our own hope. I got through it fine until the final blessing. And then the *finality* of it hit me. It wasn't the grave, it was the final blessing, the final goodbye at the Mass, when I saw the casket being wheeled down the aisle. That's when it got to me. That was the one moment when it really hit me very emotionally that it was *over*. It was *done*. I'd never see my mother again."

Cynthia Sanderson describes a similar experience: "What I remember is the casket being lowered into the grave. I was amazed at how deep the hole was. I'd never known that. That was the thing: seeing the coffin going into the ground made it totally real. Final. The Jewish custom is that the men in the family all shovel in some dirt onto the coffin. And the *sound* of the dirt hitting the coffin: first of all how *long* it took to get there, how deep down it is; and then the sound of it hitting."

These are unquestionably difficult experiences. There's no point in pretending otherwise. But what can be more difficult is the *absence* of a realization—a realization touching you on the deepest level—that your parent has died. This kind of realization is often difficult to reach, especially in the aftermath of a sudden death. The funeral can be important to you even if only for this reason.

But funerals serve another purpose: they can reassure you about your sense of belonging. If your parent's death has left you feeling weary and disconnected from your friends and relatives, the funeral can be helpful in reestablishing your common ground with them. Birgit A., fifty-eight, who was forty-eight when her eighty-four-year-old father died, found that "When I went to the funeral, I remember feeling almost a little detached. It was as if I had said goodbye to my dad a long time before. But it became really more a time just to be with the rest of the family. There was some joy in that, and in sharing old experiences and that sort of thing. The funeral had a very intimate feeling of sharing with the other family members."

Other mourning rituals provide similar experiences. The Catholic tradition of the wake, though sometimes an object of criticism, nonetheless provides an important opportunity for shared grieving. The Jewish tradition of "sitting *shiva*"— a seven-day period during which friends and relatives visit the bereaved at their home—serves a similar function over a more extended period of time. In describing her family's experience of sitting *shiva*, Deborah N. says, "For us, it was a wonderful thing. My sister came. Our families came. Friends dropped in for the first few nights. It was good that we had this, because it allowed us to laugh and cry and reminisce—all the good things that we needed to do. The crying together was a wonderful experience. When it was over, we had to return to the regular ups and downs of living." (Deborah is fifty-six; she was forty-seven when her father died at age seventy-eight.)

During the last several decades, however, many Americans have decided that customs like the wake, sitting *shiva,* and funerals themselves are pointless, even tasteless. People feel less obliged to attend funerals than before. Families may arrange only the most limited ceremonies for their relatives. Certainly these attitudes reflect legitimate concerns. Commercialism within the funeral industry has inspired a backlash against extravagant funerals, and the general easing of social obligations throughout American culture has prompted many people to pay less attention to what were often oppressive mourning rites.

Still, there's a risk of discarding valuable customs along with some that may be expendable. Robert Fulton of the Center for Death Education and Research believes that more and more Americans are "repulsed by traditional funeral practices" and are even less likely to arrange them for a deceased parent than for other relatives. But as a result of these trends, Dr. Fulton worries that our culture may deprive many Americans of significant rites of passage. "As social ceremonies that bring together a relatively large group of family members and friends," he and his colleagues Greg Owen and Eric Markusen have written in a recent article, "funerals are important socialization experiences. . . . The impulse to exclude . . . funerals from society may have unintended consequences." Among these consequences are limiting children's opportunities to learn about one of life's basic realities, and limiting the middle generation's chance to ceremonialize the passing of the elderly.

There's no question that traditional funerals *potentially* serve an important purpose: to help you feel and express grief and loss. There's also no question that traditional funerals don't *necessarily* serve this purpose. You and your family may have other preferences for expressing emotional needs. If you consider funerals repulsive or offensive, then you certainly shouldn't feel obliged to arrange one for your parent. (Your parent's wishes in this regard will be an important consideration, however.) But does this mean that you should dispense with ceremony altogether? Isn't there a means of sharing bereavement in a more flexible, less tradition-bound way?

One possibility is to borrow a custom from the Society of Friends—the Quakers. For centuries, the Quakers have memorialized the dead in a way that people from other traditions could adapt to their own purposes, in accordance with their own beliefs, and in their own style. The ceremony involves a gathering of relatives and friends who, following an initial period of silence, take turns recalling that person and what he or she meant to them, to their families, to the community. In addition to acknowledging the person's death, this custom celebrates the life and its effects on the living.

My family arranged a gathering of this sort a few days after my dad's death. Actually, "arranged" makes it sound more structured and formal than it was; with the exception of notifying the people involved a day or two in advance, there was no planning whatever. We got somewhat rowdier than most Quakers would have, but there was a definite ceremonial sense to the occasion. We prepared some of Codger's favorite foods, we built a fire in the fireplace, and we opened a bottle or two of his favorite wine. Then we proceeded to tell as many "Codger stories" as we wanted—each person speaking simply as the whim arose. Some of the stories were touching, some sad, some funny, many of them all these things at once. Their variety reflected the complexity of our feelings at the time. I remember being quietly upset throughout the whole gathering. But in its own way, that afternoon was wonderful. It was a kind of *bon voyage* party. It hurt to be saying goodbye, but we needed to do it, and it was best to be doing so together.

As regards specifically practical matters, it's worth noting that there are several good alternatives to traditional funerals. A variety of information services can help you make the decisions facing you. The National Funeral Directors Association provides a series of pamphlets describing different aspects of funerals, including cost and professional ethics. The Continental Association of Funeral and Memorial Societies offers a list of member organizations formed "to obtain dignity, simplicity and economy in funeral arrangements." See Appendix B for names and addresses of these organizations. In addition, most churches and synagogues have information about available services in your community.

Estates—Salt in the Wound

Besides the funeral, probably the most difficult immediate situation facing you will be settling your parent's estate. Estates have two fundamental dimensions. One of them, unfortunately, is the legal dimension. If you haven't had your fill of bureaucracy by this point, here's your chance to drink deep at the well of rigmarole. The other dimension—often ignored or not even acknowledged—is emotional.

Legal Dimension of Estates

The procedures involved in settling estates are so complex and vary so widely from state to state that this book can't even start to discuss them adequately. However, certain books can give you an overview of the probate process. *How to Avoid Probate!*, by Norman F. Dacey, is a massive compendium of information, advice, and sample documents for working with estates. This book emphasizes estate planning. Given your probable situation, an emphasis on planning may be less than ideal; however, the straightforward descriptions and the abundance of tips in Norman Dacey's book can at least serve as a map to the probate labyrinth. Barbara R. Stock's *It's Easy to Avoid Probate and Guardianships* offers similar information in a more compact form. Another helpful sourcebook is *The Essential Guide to Wills, Estates, Trusts, and Death Taxes*, by Alex J. Soled. See Appendix C for details on these and other books about estates.

Emotional Dimension of Estates

No matter how complex, however, the legal dimension of estates isn't the whole story. There's also the emotional dimension—the psychological consequences of the legal and financial tasks facing you. Depending on your personal and family situations, this emotional dimension may actually prove as difficult as the legal one.

There are several reasons why. One is simply that settling an estate is long and often frustrating work. The months or years of dealing with legal issues can exhaust you both physically and emotionally. Estates can also create tensions and resentments within your family. In addition, long delays in settling an estate can prolong or delay your bereavement process. The situation is ironic: although your parents intended your inheritance to help you after their deaths—perhaps even to offer a degree of consolation—the estate may end up salt in the wound.

Although bureaucratic delays are the biggest frustration for most people, sometimes even the final settlement is fraught with problems. Leona N., sixty-two (she was sixty when her parents died at eighty-five and eighty-six), received an inheritance that became more and more troublesome. "I inherited fourteen hundred acres of land which has been running downhill for a long time," she explains. "It was assessed at the value of the land at the time [of her parents' deaths], which is *way* over what I could sell it for now. And so I had to borrow a hundred thousand dollars to pay the taxes, and I've been paying on that interest ever since, while unable to sell the land."

The land that Leona inherited has continued to cause her financial and legal trouble. "I've paid many thousands of dollars in lawyers' fees to sort out the problems. The amount of stocks I inherited has nowhere near touched the cost of even the interest on my loans. It's been just a big drain." But her difficulty is not just legal and financial. Leona herself admits that "It's kind of an awful thing that I seem unable to resolve. It really is as though I haven't buried my father yet." Leona's inheritance is much more than just geographical and financial; it's also a psychological legacy— perhaps a sense of obligation to her parent's wishes and expectations, or perhaps an inability to part with their treasured possession.

If you find yourself in a similar situation—even with lower financial stakes—you should consider the following questions:

- What are the issues involved in this estate?
- Specifically, which issues are financial, which are legal, and which are psychological?
- Are you possibly confusing them? Are you mistaking certain emotional issues (such as doing what your parent "would have wanted" you to do) for financial or legal issues (such as deciding to keep or rent or sell the family house)?

These questions appear to be simple and straightforward. In fact, they may be extremely difficult to answer. But without answering them carefully (and as early as possible) you may find your inheritance more of a burden than a blessing.

Another possible consequence of an inheritance is that your inheritance may seem tainted. You may feel guilty or sad because money or other bequests reached you as a result of your parent's death. Winnie C., for instance, inherited large sums of money when her sixty-two-year-old mother died. (Winnie was thirty-five at the time; she is thirty-eight now.) "I did not handle the money well," she says. "I felt quite a bit of guilt about it, especially because I was the lone survivor." Joyce E., who is forty-six (she was thirty-five when her father died at seventy, thirty-six when her mother died at sixty-eight), felt "uncomfortable with inheriting the retirement savings of a lifetime—which my parents had never had time to use."

Guilt can also result from your feeling that you didn't "do enough" for your parent, or that didn't do what you did with perfect motives. Such feelings may be especially intense in the aftermath of decisions to cease aggressive medical care, or to cease treatment altogether. Jack and Marge N. faced these issues last year when Jack's ninety-one-year-old mother pleaded for help in fasting to death. "Because we benefited from her death both physically [freedom from having to care for her] and financially," Jack says, "we had to question our motives for helping her die." A financial windfall under these circumstances can make you doubt what were in fact selfless motives.

But keep in mind that situations of this sort, though regrettable, are probably not your fault. You didn't want your parent to take ill. You didn't want your parent (and you yourself) to struggle with complex medical decisions. You didn't want your parent to die. Yet financial, medical, moral, and interpersonal issues tend to get hopelessly entangled. You can't always keep them separate. Perhaps your only recourse is to avoid jumbling them together without good reason. The likelihood is that you acted as thoughtfully and generously as possible under the circumstances. Your inheritance is an unrelated issue. Don't question your motives without good cause.

Why not think of your inheritance as a final gift—a way that your parents have done one last thing to help you materially, just as they helped you many times throughout your life? Perhaps the real decision is what use to make of the inheritance. Sometimes that has been decided in advance, whether through a trust or through other stipulations. Sometimes your own financial situation settles the issue. But perhaps your inheritance can allow you to do something that would have been impossible otherwise. Just as your parents' other gifts—both material and intangible—made possible other stages of your development, perhaps an inheritance can provide the financial backing for a new stage now.

One last matter. Many parents appoint an adult son or daughter as executor of the estate. This procedure makes sense in many ways; however, it also gives rise to more problems than perhaps any other aspect of estates. As Avery D., forty-two, says about the legal aftermath of his sixty-two-year-old mother's death two years ago: "The appointment of an heir as executor is not recommended. It is too close to being a conflict of interest, at least in the eyes of the other heirs."

Your Parent's Personal Belongings

If your other parent is still alive, then he or she will probably inherit everything from the parent who died. If both parents are now dead, however, the decisions facing you will be more complicated. You and your siblings or other relatives may have to determine what happens to your parents' estate, including all personal belongings—and may have to decide within a short while.

Several aspects of the situation make it potentially problematic. One of them, as usual, is probate. You may have to wait for the court's decision before making any specific plans. But once the legal process is complete, the interpersonal process remains. And although dividing up a parent's personal belongings needn't be a problem, sometimes it turns out that way.

Most brothers and sisters work through the distribution of their parent's belongings without major difficulties. "When we divided up all the household things after my father died, there was not one moment of conflict among us four kids," according to Simon R. (He is sixty-five; he was twenty-five when his sixty-two-year-old mother died, twenty-seven when his sixty-seven-year-old father died.) "If I wanted that picture, it was mine. If my sister wanted that silver tray, it was hers. The four of us did it with no effort and with lots of appreciation." Similarly, Leonard U., fifty-three (twenty-five when his father died at fifty-seven, fifty when his mother died at eighty), found that "When we were giving Mother's personal things away, there was more difficulty in getting each other to accept something than in wanting something for ourselves. That brought us closer together, although we had always been close anyway."

But others aren't so lucky. Even when siblings get along, the distribution of a parent's personal effects can trigger all sorts of misunderstandings. Mark Cernik describes an awkward experience when he and his siblings divided up their mother's possessions. All of Mark's siblings are married and have children; Mark, however, is single. Mark has established his own life as a single adult, but he feels that his bonds to his mother, to his hometown, and even to the family house had remained stronger over the years than what his siblings felt. As it turned out, dividing up the possessions affected him differently from how it affected the others. Mark explains, "I was sitting in the living room of my mother's house, and my siblings were dividing things up, as I was, too. And I remember that what struck me was: 'You all are dividing things up to take to your houses. But what you're dividing up was *my home.* And it's all disappearing before my eyes.'"

The problem is rarely a matter of greed. It's usually more the belongings' sentimental value. Perhaps you and your siblings feel strongly about keeping the same item. Or else one sibling wants to keep an item, but you want to sell it. To argue over the dollar value of belongings is beside the point. The values in question are unpredictable—sometimes almost irrational. Moreover, what appear to be conflicts over material possessions may originate in older, complex sibling rivalries. As Harvard sociologist Robert Weiss sums up the situation, "The siblings who have real trouble are the people whose unclear inheritances provide a vehicle for expressing other tensions." Although severe conflicts are unusual, disagreements can erupt and create hard feelings for everyone.

Sometimes the situation goes to ludicrous extremes. Dr. Fulton tells a story about one parent's favorite piece of furniture: "A brother and sister went all the way to the Supreme Court arguing over a rocking chair. It was an extraordinarily wealthy family. They had millions of dollars. They didn't want to do anything with the estate, though—wouldn't sign a paper or settle anything—until they first took the rocking chair to the Supreme Court. A Solomonlike judge determined that the daughter could get the rocking chair for six months; then the son could get it. They would take turns. But there was to be no change, no painting, no alterations of this rocking chair whatsoever."

How should you deal with distributing your parent's possessions? You certainly won't end up needing the nine eminent justices to help. You and your siblings will probably just work it out. But if you can't, and if tempers rise and accusations fly, then you should devise some sort of alternative as soon as possible. One possibility is to ask a trusted relative or family friend to mediate. Accepting a sympathetic, evenhanded outside opinion can save you expense and trouble in the long run.

One other possible problem: remaining clearheaded over the belongings you inherit. Some people feel a temptation either to hang on to their parent's personal effects desperately or to dispose of them impulsively. Neither course of action is a disaster. Still, the intense emotions following a parent's death can prompt you to make decisions that you'll regret later.

For instance, you may decide to make a "clean sweep" after the death—selling your parent's house, furniture, knickknacks, the works. Sometimes financial problems or family obligations rule out any other approach. And of course a houseful of accumulated possessions can become a headache in its own right. Even so, it may be worth the effort to hold off a while, to consider the alternatives, to see how the situation affects you before you act on it. This holds true even for lesser inheritances, such as your share of personal effects. But it's especially important when you deal with a family house or other real estate.

Audrey D., who is thirty-nine (she was thirty-seven when her father died at seventy-two), ran into trouble after she and her sister inherited their father's house. Initially, they rented out the house for a year rather than selling it. This interval gave them time to decide on a course of action. Later, the sisters sold the house. Audrey then sorted through the family furnishings and her father's personal effects. "I found it wonderful to say goodbye to my home," Audrey explains, "and to savor its memories when I went back to clear it out a year after Dad died. A year helped a lot."

Yet she encountered some difficulties along the way. One problem was that in getting the house ready to rent, Audrey cleared it out more thoroughly than she wished she had later. She says, "In our haste, we threw out some things we should have looked at more carefully." Even a year later, the practical task of clearing the house was still emotionally charged. "I was alone doing the work—my sister had to go back to her job in France. So I stayed by myself. This was fine in some ways, but going through things by myself was the loneliest thing I've ever done. I think people should have someone special around when they're 'sorting out a lifetime.'"

It's also advisable to consider the long-term emotional consequences of what may appear to be only short-term practical decisions. Rubie O., who is thirty-two, was twenty-seven when her fifty-six-year-old mother died. She and her siblings inherited a vacation house on a lake—the site of many family get-togethers. "After four years," Rubie explains, "we realized that we couldn't keep up the 'shore house'; it had become a burden. The burden was more time-consuming than financial. We sold the house. So now we are without a summer house for get-togethers, and I see this as a major mistake. I don't believe all the kids will now get together as regularly." Although situations of this sort may seem less than crucial at the time, deciding how to deal with them hastily can have unexpected consequences—not just for you alone, but for you in relation to your whole family.

On the other hand, you may feel that keeping what you received from your parent is a burdensome reminder of hard times you now wish to forget. You should follow your own hunches in this regard. Generally, what goes and what stays will probably sort itself out. Possessions often fall by the wayside when we cease to need them. Although a few people run the risk of a kind of "shrine mentality" toward their parents—maintaining the house just as it was, or keeping every last article of clothing—this is a rare problem. For most people, there's little risk in keeping whatever you want. There's more danger in discarding possessions that you might want back later.

Lawsuits

Like the subject of estates, the issue of lawsuits following a parent's death is too complex and too varied for detailed discussion in this book. But the psychological dimension is appropriate for discussion here.

The circumstances of your parent's death may convince you that you have a personal, moral, or financial need to sue a doctor, a hospital, or some other individual or institution. Perhaps you have good reasons for doing so. Before proceeding, however, ask yourself two questions.

First, is it possible that taking legal action expresses a sentiment *other* than a sense of ethical outrage toward your parent's death—perhaps a sense of outrage at the loss you have suffered, at your helplessness during a crisis, or even at death itself? Perhaps medical personnel or institutions did, in fact, contribute to your parent's suffering or death. But perhaps what happened was more a result of human limitations than of negligence or malpractice. This is not to say that your anger and sadness are inappropriate. Watching someone suffer and die *is* infuriating. But perhaps the anger you feel has no single legitimate target. We Americans often assume that someone deserves the ultimate credit or blame for everything. *Someone* must take responsibility! But perhaps sometimes there is no negligence or malpractice as such, but only human fallibility and human mortality. In short, your outrage may be appropriate but misdirected.

Second, even if legal action is appropriate, is it worth the possible trauma that can result? Perhaps it is. Sometimes you have to take a stand regardless of the emotional and financial cost. But you should consider the possible consequences. A medical malpractice suit can drag on for years. Although your lawyers will probably charge you on a contingency basis (that is, according to a percentage of any award in your favor), there may be other expenses along the way, including time away from your work and travel costs for you or other family members living away from wherever the case will be tried. These expenses can add up fast.

The emotional costs can be still higher. The months—or, more likely, the years—that a suit takes to reach the courts can create uncertainty in the lives of everyone involved. Such uncertainty isn't just a matter of waiting for the outcome. In addition, the sense of suspension that often results from lawsuits can slow or disrupt your recovery from bereavement. Just as a parent's protracted illness can create a feeling of being "on hold," a lingering lawsuit can limit your ability to get back to normal. You may not even start to grieve until the verdict is in. If the verdict is not in your favor, the subsequent letdown may complicate the bereavement process still further.

How should you proceed? Here, as in other aspects of dealing with loss, there is no simple answer. Perhaps righting a medical wrong takes precedence over returning to a normal life. In the aftermath of an unjust or unnecessary death, you may not even be *able* to live a normal life. Perhaps, however, your family's situation rules out wrestling with these legal issues. If your surviving parent is elderly or sick, you may not have the time (let alone the will) for legal battles. Deciding how to proceed is difficult.

One possibility is to wait a while before making a decision. Most states have a statute of limitations on medical malpractice suits; determining the time limit will at least give you a sense of how long you have before deciding your course of action. (You should, of course, record all the details of the case as soon as possible after its occurrence. Don't trust your memory to retain these details.) Another possibility is to obtain a second legal opinion on the case. The expense of acquiring objective legal advice will be a fraction of what a lawsuit could cost you.

Other Tasks Following a Parent's Death

In closing, let's touch on a scattering of tasks that you may have to face. You may not have to contend with all of them, but they're easy to forget in the flurry of activity that often follows a parent's death.

1. Decide on a time and place for the funeral or memorial service.
2. Make a list of immediate family, close friends, and employers or business colleagues. Notify each person by phone.
3. Write an obituary, if necessary. (Many funeral directors perform this service.) Include age, place of birth, cause of death, occupation, college degrees, memberships held, military service, outstanding work, list of survivors within the immediate family. Give the time and place of services. Contact newspapers to provide information.

4. Locate insurance policies. Notify insurance companies.
5. Locate the will. Notify the lawyer and executor.
6. Arrange for members of the family or close friends to take turns answering the door or phone. Keep careful record of all calls.
7. Arrange appropriate child care.
8. Coordinate supplying of food for the next several days.
9. Consider special needs for the household—cleaning, etc.—that friends might help with.
10. Arrange lodging for visiting relatives and friends.
11. Select pallbearers and notify them.
12. If you are omitting flowers from the service, decide on an appropriate memorial for donations (such as a church, library, school, or charity).
13. If you are accepting flowers, plan for their disposition after the service (hospital, nursing home, or other institution).
14. Prepare a list of distant relatives or friends to notify by letter or printed notice.
15. Prepare copy for printed notice, if needed.
16. Prepare a list of persons to acknowledge for calls, flowers, etc. Send appropriate acknowledgments, whether in the form of notes or printed cards. (Note: many funeral directors perform this service.)
17. Check all life and casualty insurance agencies, including Social Security, credit union, trade union, and fraternal or military organizations. Check on income for survivors from these sources. Notify companies or agencies.
18. Check promptly on all debts and installment payments. Some may carry insurance clauses that will cancel them. If there will be a delay in meeting payments, consult with creditors and ask for more time before the payments are due.

19. If the deceased was living alone, notify utilities and landlord. Notify the post office also.

This list is adapted from Ernest Morgan, ed., *A Manual of Death Education and Simple Burial* (Burnsville, N.C.: Celo Press, 1977).

Having looked at the practical tasks most likely to affect you after a parent's death, let's now examine the likeliest emotional and interpersonal issues. The following chapter will consider family changes. Chapter Eight will explore personal changes.

SEVEN

FAMILY CHANGES

The previous chapter suggested at one point that certain events following your parent's death can strain relationships with family members. However, the strains are not just a result of practical issues like estates and lawsuits. A parent's death can also challenge you in more fundamental ways. The reason isn't hard to identify. After all, your parent's death has changed your family's structure and your family members' ways of interacting.

Sometimes there's no effect beyond the most obvious and immediate change—your parent's absence from the family. But the death can change your family in ways that go far beyond the loss of a single member. You may end up growing closer to your other parent, or you may drift away. You and your brothers and sisters may rediscover each other after years of mutual indifference, or you may become estranged. Your whole family may reconcile its differences, or you may cease interacting at all. And of course a whole range of other, subtler changes may occur as well.

Your Relationship with Your Surviving Parent

The death of one parent is often a major turning-point in dealing with the other. Sometimes tremendous growth occurs—renewing of ties, deepening of appreciation, and intensifying of love. Unfortunately, the result is sometimes less favorable—deteriorating of bonds, heightening of resentments, fading of affection. In addition, one parent's death can alter your responsibilities toward the other, with either positive or negative effects on your relationship.

New Closeness

Shared loss can bring both you and your parent to a realization that time is short and that old misunderstandings shouldn't keep you from sharing whatever you have in common. The loss of one parent can inspire you to work toward a deeper relationship. These insights and the changes they can produce are among the great consolations for a parent's death.

Winnie C., thirty-eight, found that "I became much closer to my mother after my father died. Although I 'parented' her a lot, we also became friends." Similarly, Claudia V., forty-two (thirty-seven when her mother died at sixty-eight), feels that "I was closer to Father after Mother's death. We had never been close before." Russell A., thirty-eight, whose sixty-two-year-old mother died this past year, says, "My father and I enjoy a much more intimate relationship. We have joined in an intense and healthy interdependence unavailable to us because of my mother's jealousy and insecurities." And Gwen S., thirty-six, who was thirty-one when her mother died at sixty-three, says, "My father and I have gotten closer. I don't think the relationship between my father and myself would ever have developed this way if my mother was still living—I would probably have continued to talk only with her."

John C. is forty-four. When he was thirty-two, his mother died at the age of fifty-one. John subsequently had a dramatic reconciliation with his long-estranged father. The loss of his mother changed many of John's attitudes, among them a sense that he and his father could never get along.

"With the encouragement of my sisters," John explains, "I started a correspondence with my father, and followed up with a visit to his home in Arkansas. It's one of the best things I ever did. We may never have the father-son relationship that others have enjoyed, but there *is* a relationship now. Maybe it's a selfish motive on my part, but I think now that when my father dies, he will die knowing that I love him, and all those old bottled-up hard feelings had been disposed of between us."

Changes of this magnitude are rare; when they happen, they rarely take place so abruptly. But they do occur. Audrey D.'s experience is perhaps more typical: "After my mother died, my dad started coming out to visit my husband and me for four to six weeks every year," Audrey explains. (She is thirty-nine; she was twenty-nine when her sixty-seven-year-old mother died.) "I hadn't spent that much time alone with him before, and I felt I got to know him better now. I was glad I had that opportunity, because I had never loved him as much as my mother. I learned to appreciate some of his finer traits, of which there were many, and to not be bothered as much by some of his faults."

What's most important is to stay receptive to changes within your relationship. New closeness is valuable no matter how subtle or obvious it may be. Just keep in mind that old attitudes and roles are durable; change may take years to occur.

Estrangements

A parent's death can draw you closer to your other parent, but it can just as easily strain your relationship instead. Lu F. discovered that her father's death harmed her already difficult relationship with her mother. (Lu is thirty-eight; she was twenty-five when her father died at the age of fifty-eight.) "Mother has had difficulty adjusting to her life without my father," she says. "This has put a strain on all the children at times. My father was the closest to me, so at times this puts my mom and me further apart." Marie W., forty-three, had a similar experience (she was thirty-two when her sixty-seven-year-old father died): "I am distant from Mom both in miles and emotionally. The gap that was always there has widened considerably. My dad was the one who was always glad to see me, and I felt totally abandoned by his death. I remember thinking, 'I will never be as welcome at home now.'" Sometimes these changes in relationships are temporary—perhaps a side effect of tensions during or right after a family crisis. At other times, they are the start of permanent estrangement.

What accounts for these disruptions? Why would family members who have already suffered one loss compound it by creating another? There are many possible explanations—some of them a result of specific issues within the families. But there are some general reasons as well.

One is that loss and bereavement are private experiences in many ways, and their emotional effects on individuals are unpredictable. No doubt you and your family members share a sense of loss. But the person who has died has a special meaning for each person within your family; each family member has an individual way of feeling and expressing his or her own sense of loss; and sometimes these differences cause conflicts instead of harmony, isolation instead of solidarity.

For instance, if your father has died, you are mourning the loss of a parent. Meanwhile, your mother is mourning the loss of her spouse. Both losses are emotionally difficult. But they are different losses in many ways. Yours is the loss of the man who helped to create you and nurture you; your mother's is the loss of the man she chose to be her mate. Although you have shared certain experiences that your father and her husband brought to your lives, your sense of that person will be drastically different. Even the experiences you shared may have different meanings for each of you.

In addition, the practical effects of the loss will differ. Adult sons and daughters often suffer few practical consequences following a parent's death. Widows, in contrast, often experience severe disruptions. For most women—especially those in the generations now fifty and older—widowhood can drastically alter not just financial well-being, but social status as well. Few sons and daughters ever contend with changes as extensive as what widows routinely face. Understanding the depth and breadth of change within a widow's life may require considerable effort and imagination by even a sympathetic son or daughter.

These matters are obvious but easy to forget. During the past fifteen years or so, Americans have come to recognize the problems of widowhood; our attitudes about widows have started to change. Yet in the aftermath of a loss, when stress is high and energy is low, it's often difficult to remember how different people's bereavement can be. The fact that both you and your surviving parent are both bereaved doesn't necessarily mean that you stand on the same ground. Likewise, sharing a loss won't necessarily make you the best persons to help each other, just as one hungry person isn't able to help another just because they both understand the pain of hunger.

Responses

Is there *anything* you can do to help? As with other aspects of bereavement, there are no simple actions that will settle everything once and for all. But here are several possible responses that can make a difference:

- **Look after your own bereavement.** You have your own loss to mourn. If you ignore your health, your feelings, your job, your spouse and children, your friendships, and other aspects of your life, you harm yourself enough to limit how much you can help others.
- **At the same time, try to be there, if possible, for your**

surviving parent. "Being there" doesn't have to mean being there physically; it doesn't even mean that you should respond to every request or demand that your father or mother makes of you. But try to remember that widowhood or widowerhood involves one of the most difficult transitions that people ever experience. Your parent's grief process will take a long time—probably longer than yours will. Patience and a willingness to listen nonjudgmentally will at least allow your parent a chance to express thoughts and emotions that other people may refuse to hear at all.

• **Recognize the limits of what you can do to help.** You can be sympathetic and supportive, but you can't take away someone else's pain. Trying to work miracles will exhaust and disappoint you. Ultimately, your parent must mourn her or his own loss, and must reconstruct a meaningful life by choice, not by others' intervention.

• **Get support for yourself and suggest separate support for your parent.** Counseling or a bereavement group can help you and your surviving parent.

One last suggestion. Keep an eye open to the possibility that your surviving parent may not deal successfully with bereavement. The death of a spouse can cause serious difficulties for the survivor. If your mother or father develops debilitating problems, you may need to suggest ways for her or him to take hold of the situation. The specific points of concern are:

• protracted inability to believe that her or his spouse has really died;
• protracted social isolation following the death;
• inability to care for herself or himself;
• reliance on alcohol or drugs to relieve a sense of anguish, loneliness, guilt, or other emotions;
• extensive changing of plans or making of decisions ac-

cording to what her or his spouse would have preferred, rather than according to personal preferences;

- great effort to *avoid* thinking of the spouse;
- substantial weight gain, weight loss, or marked deterioration of health;
- suicidal thoughts or gestures, or attempted suicide;
- inability to "get on" with life, to invest energy in living.

How well your parent is actually dealing with bereavement is often hard to determine. This would be true even if bereavement were the only issue at the time. Unfortunately, you may have to determine whether your surviving parent is at risk in other ways as well. The perceptions of relatives or family friends can be helpful in this regard.

Increased Responsibilities

If your parent is ill or unable to care for himself or herself, you may find your family responsibilities changing when your first parent dies. Even if your surviving parent is still in good health, however, you may find your role changing in certain respects.

The crux of the matter in such situations is to take stock of the situation and to marshal your resources as fully as possible. Here are some suggestions for how to proceed:

- **Determine how you can share responsibilities with siblings and other relatives.** There may be no reason for you to carry the whole weight yourself. Your relatives may want and *need* to carry their own share. Reluctant relatives are a problem, of course, but considering them unable or unwilling to help from the outset will do a disservice to everyone involved. Full discussion of the issues, though potentially awkward, may spare you time, effort, and trouble in the future.
- **Explore all possible resources available to your family.** Depending on your surviving parent's age, state of health, financial situation, and personal preferences,

there may be agencies or individuals able to help you. The National Support Center for Families of the Aging, Children of Aging Parents, the National Self-Help Clearinghouse, the National Hospice Organization, and other information centers can direct you to suitable resources. See Appendix B for further details.

- **Discuss these issues with your parent.** After all, it's his or her life that's the chief issue. Your parent may need help, but he or she has to take responsibilities, too. It's important that you understand each other's thoughts and feelings about the changes within your family. Attitudes that "one simply doesn't discuss such matters"—whether regarding finances, medical insurance, wills, or other matters—can cause great damage in the long run. For instance, arranging a power-of-attorney *before* a medical crisis is crucial; waiting till afterward may be too late. The same holds true for other financial arrangements, estate planning, and ethical concerns surrounding "living wills" and hospital care.

- **Don't feel that you are the only source of all good or ill that befalls your parent.** You will all be better off for dealing with these issues in advance. If your parent is unable or unwilling to make decisions about her or his own well-being, you'll have to respond as imaginatively as possible. But you're not the ultimate source of your parent's happiness or misery. It's regrettable but true that some widows and widowers never regain the sense of purpose or well-being that they felt before their spouse's death. You can't *make* your parent decide how she or he should live this new phase of life. Don't try to change what may be decades-old patterns of behavior.

Relations with Siblings

Just as sons and daughters sometimes grow closer or less close to their surviving parents following a loss, brothers and sisters can strengthen or weaken their relationships. Your second parent's death, especially, may prompt you and your siblings to reconsider what you mean to each other. Sometimes new attitudes forge new bonds. Yet your parent's death may harm your relationships with your siblings as well.

New Closeness

Next to your parents, your siblings are probably the people you have known longest. You may not be in close contact with them anymore; you may not get along with them; you may not even *like* them; but you probably feel that you share something with them that you share with no one else. You share your origins. You share your parents. You share several decades of your past. When your parents die, it's hard not to feel that you're all in the same situation. You're losing a parent—the *same* parent. So aren't you the best people to understand each other and assist each other during the crisis?

Sometimes it works out that way. Susan C. and Hannah G. are sisters, fifty-one and fifty-three years old respectively. When their seventy-five-year-old mother died last year, the sisters found that they were each other's emotional salvation. Susan says, "Hannah and I have always been very close, but Mother's death allows us to express our sad emotional feelings with each other. Hannah and I speak about how we feel, how empty we both feel. We can cry together. We worked together, and we were lucky to have each other."

Other siblings have felt less close before their parents die, but draw closer following the shared loss. Karen N., who is forty (she was eighteen when her father died at forty-two, twenty-nine when her mother died at fifty-four), says of her brothers, "After my mother's death, we became closer because we did not have parents who were alive." Jon L., forty-two, whose parents died recently at the ages of sixty-nine and seventy-two, had a similar experience: "My sisters and I stuck close together after Mother's death, and we have gotten closer after Father's." At times, the change can approach transformation: Beryl J., twenty-two (twenty when her mother died at age fifty), found that "Our family life has improved. My relationship with my younger sister is absolutely beautiful."

These changes, like those that can occur between you and your surviving parent, seem a consequence of what we might call "mortality shock." As Gwen S., thirty-six, says about her sixty-three-year-old mother's death five years ago: "I think it made me realize how temporary our relationships can be and made me more appreciative of them." Siblings are lucky when they reach this kind of realization. Death can deprive us of the people we love, but it can also help us to discover them.

Estrangement from Siblings

But parental loss and its effects can also disrupt or even destroy your sibling relationships. Discord between siblings following a parent's death is regrettably common.

Lack of cooperation during the crisis is probably the commonest sore point. Perhaps certain brothers and sisters provided care and others didn't, for example. "Often, given our mobile society, there may be only one adult child near the parent," according to Wendy Foster-Evans of the Hospice of Marin. "Everybody else may be scattered around the country with their own family commitments. So those people sort of breeze in and 'do their thing' and then breeze out. It may be that the one who is there is kind of stuck, and may feel a lot of resentment. He or she may feel some loneliness at being in that position and feeling abandoned by the rest of the family."

Matt V., fifty-nine (he was fifty-three when his eighty-two-year-old mother died), felt that "Lack of assistance from my only brother created a rather hard feeling." Sally B., thirty-nine (twenty-three when her mother died at sixty-three), experienced conflicts with both sisters: "I got mad at my sister who lives out of town for leaving all of 'it' to me. The other sister [local] worked full time, so I got all the problems." Sometimes a parent's death alters the family so extensively that siblings cease to interact at all. Anna D.'s experience was especially disruptive: "My brother was not available for the moral strength and decision-making required of me. I resent him for this—he almost completely deserted me at the time of Mother's short illness and death. He went fishing the afternoon of her funeral and the next day while I closed up her apartment and sorted out her belongings. I am sure this was the only way he could handle things. But I am still angry."

These conflicts are less surprising than they seem. Brothers and sisters who get along during a parent's illness and after the death aren't unusual, but neither are siblings who end up bickering or resenting each other. High expectations of brotherly-sisterly love probably complicate the situation. But the fact of the matter is that ironically, you and your siblings may be the last people capable of helping each other. This isn't *in spite of* the shared loss, but *because* of it. The fact is, you and your siblings are suffering the same loss. You are probably experiencing similar anxieties and stresses. You are physically or emotionally depleted in the same ways. Why should you be the perfect allies during your struggle? What each of you wants and needs—an optimistic outlook, patience, clear perspective, and abundant energy— is precisely what each of you lacks.

In addition, your parent's illness and death may evoke long-forgotten (or perhaps well-remembered) childhood competition and resentment. Dr. Raphael believes that "The conflicts may be reawakened from sibling conflicts of rivalry and envy in early childhood. The death seems to highlight what has had to be shared in caring for the parent and what burdens must be borne, and also who feels responsible." Powerful old feelings combine with the more immediate tensions. The result is a strain on sibling relationships. It's not surprising that brothers and sisters have difficulties getting along when parents die.

Responses

What should you do about these conflicts? Here are a few suggestions:

- **Remember that grief heightens emotions.** You and your siblings are under stress, and your reactions even to everyday events may be more intense than usual. What seem like insoluble problems may look easier to solve in a few months. Don't burn your bridges.
- **Try to keep issues separate.** A conflict over a seemingly practical issue (such as selling the family house) may have deep emotional roots. If you can perceive where one issue ends and another starts, you'll have a better chance of dealing with them successfully.
- **Consider the possibility of an outsider's viewpoint.** You and your siblings may have such strong feelings about the aftermath of your parent's death that you may not be able to see events clearly. A trusted aunt, uncle, other relative, or family friend may be able to provide insights that all of you lack.
- **Be careful of speaking your mind too impulsively.** Bereavement can provide an opportunity for speaking with rare candor—an opportunity often well worth taking. Ultimatums, dares, and threats during a time of confusion, however, may drastically compound the damage your family has already suffered.

Changes in Other Relationships

Although parental loss seems most likely to affect your relationships with your siblings and with your surviving parent, it may also change your relationships with other people as well. Interactions with your spouse and children may benefit or suffer from the consequences of a parent's illness and death. Even friendships may improve or deteriorate because of the stresses they undergo during your grief process.

Between You and Your Spouse

As with changes within other relationships, those that affect spouses can be favorable, unfavorable, or ambiguous. Sometimes the mortality shock following a parent's death can strengthen a marriage. Helen T. is thirty-seven (she was thirty-four when her father died at fifty-nine; thirty-seven when her mother died at sixty-one). Following her parents' deaths, Helen discovered that the losses heightened a sense of how much her marriage meant to her: "My husband is more dear to me now than anything else." Susan T., who was thirty-six when her sixty-nine-year-old father died a year ago, felt that her husband's reactions to her loss strengthened her marriage because "My husband has always been very supportive about my relationship with my parents and my father's death."

Yet when parental loss harms a marriage, the damage can be severe. "The illness caused competition for attention, and it increased discord and tension," Patricia L. says of what happened between her and her husband during her mother's long illness. (She is thirty-six; she was twenty-seven when her father died at sixty-two, twenty-nine when her mother died at sixty-one.) "My marriage began to falter. If Mother's death had not occurred within the next few months, the marriage probably would not have survived." Jacqueline E., who is forty, lost both her parents (ages seventy-seven and seventy-eight) this past year. During her parents' long illnesses, "The situation placed stress on my marriage. For though my husband was very supportive, we had little time or privacy to nurture our relationship. Only when my mother went to the nursing home and we were alone in the house again did we begin to feel how much we had been stressed and separated." Helen T. also felt that her marriage suffered from the consequences of a parent's long illness. (She is forty-four; she was forty-three when her father died at the age of eighty-one.) "My husband wanted me to be available to him," she says. "It was hard for me to divide my life so totally."

Between You and Your Children

Relationships between you and your children are less likely to suffer damage in these situations than are other bonds. A few people I've interviewed felt that their children seemed impatient with their plight—for example, Sue D., forty-five, who found that "My children could not understand why I felt such pain" following her father's death. (She was thirty-eight when he died at the age of seventy.) But most people who mentioned changes spoke of them as improvements—greater closeness with their children, increased sensitivity for their feelings, and a heightened valuing of time together.

One reason for this change is simply that parents and children have often found their family routines disrupted during a parent's illness. Getting back to normal is a relief. But another reason is the intense appreciation of life that bereavement often produces. Helen T. feels that her relationships with her children improved "because losing someone I loved so very much has made me appreciate my children even more." Doreen Y. expresses a similar sentiment: "My time with my children is more important than ever, and we are becoming extremely close."

You may have to deal with another aspect of the situation, however. If you have children who were close to their grandparents, your children will also experience bereavement. You may have to deal with their grief as well as your own. Ironically, this may help you, not hinder you, in coming to terms with your loss. Kids are usually open to feelings of grief and sadness. Their grieving for their grandparents may make your grieving for your parents easier. Sarah B. is forty-seven; she was forty-two when her mother died at seventy-five, forty-three when her father died at seventy-nine. Of her situation with her children, she says that they "continue to express thoughts about their 'missing Grandpa' often. Their memories seem to be mostly positive ones. The conversations that follow I find to be healing." At the same time, if you are having an intense reaction to your parent's deaths, you should be careful not to overwhelm your kids with your own grief. But the likelihood is that if you respect and accept your children's feelings, the situation will allow everyone a chance to share the sense of loss.

Between You and Your Friends

Even relationships with friends can benefit or suffer from your bereavement. Friendship ties may be different from those with your relatives, but grief can affect them anyway. The difficulties you face in dealing with a parent's death and your subsequent bereavement can actually make or break friendships. As Sue N. put it, "You do find out who your *real* friends are! The desire of most of my 'friends' not to talk with me about Mom's death was very hard to deal with. I even had one such 'friend' sever our relationship totally!" According to Paula T., "The experience intensified the quality of my relationships." (She is forty-four; she was thirty-one when her father died at fifty-eight; thirty-seven when her mother died at sixty-two.) "Marginal friendships either became very meaningful or died."

What about improvements? They aren't uncommon. Joanne Q., sixty, who was fifty when her father died at eighty-two, felt "appreciative of my friends' concern," and long-term benefits resulted in several friendships. Claudia V. felt a "close bond with friends in the same situation." (She is forty-two; she was thirty-seven when her sixty-eight-year-old mother died, forty when her sixty-eight-year-old father died.) Susan T., thirty-three (she was twenty-eight when her mother died at sixty-three), found that losing a parent actually strengthened friendships because her own capacities for compassion had increased. "I feel I can offer more comfort when they have to face their parent's death, since I've been through it," she explains.

The suggestions made earlier about your siblings or parents apply to these relationships as well—at least to some extent. Loss and grief can change friendships and other bonds, but the effects diminish over time. Over the next few months and years, your relationships will return to a more balanced state. If it's any consolation, many people seem to find positive changes occurring in their relationships more often than negative ones. Your marriage and parent-child relationships are unlikely to suffer permanent damage following your parent's death. Friendships are somewhat less predictable. It's a real loss when friendships fall by the wayside. But some friendships may grow stronger even if others weaken. Either way, the changes are not entirely your choice. Your friends must make some sort of effort, too, in understanding and accepting the changes in your life.

All Quiet on the Family Front

One other possibility: perhaps, following your parent's death, no relationships will change at all, or will change just minimally. Many adult sons and daughters find that their lives remain much the same after parental loss. They are neither closer to their relatives and friends nor estranged from them. In particular, some men seem relatively unaffected by the aftermath.

Whatever the reason, there's certainly no reason for you to feel that changes *must* occur between you and the people close to you following your parent's death. When the boat isn't rocking, just sit back and count yourself lucky.

EIGHT

PERSONAL CHANGES

Listen to these voices:

"I was hurt and confused by everything that happened both during my mother's illness and after her death."
—Bernice J., twenty-eight (twenty-five when her mother died at fifty-five)

"No big change in my life besides the normal grief associated with the loss of a mother and father. Living some distance from them and having my own wife and family provided a cushion for my loss."
—Ben K., sixty-nine (forty-seven when his mother died at seventy-one; fifty when his father died at seventy-four)

"I felt a deep loss, but coped fairly well because of memories of many good times from childhood."
—Amanda F., fifty (forty-six when her father died at seventy-two)

"Experiencing my father's death very much affected my life. Every moment became much more meaningful, as I realized that the moment is all that we really have. Experiencing and expressing love have become the only vital elements in life."
—Doreen Y., thirty-six (thirty-one when her father died at fifty-seven)

These statements are just a sampling of the enormous variety of ways that a parent's death can affect adult sons and daughters. But they should suggest that in fact many outcomes are possible: trauma, transformation, and a full range of alternatives in between. Most people probably experience a mixture of changes in their lives—a balance of favorable and unfavorable effects—rather than any particular extreme. But usually a parent's death causes *some* sort of personal change.

Further Emotional Experiences

In addition to the aspects of emotions already discussed in Chapter Two—namely, the intensity and variety of feelings that can occur throughout the grief process—some other aspects may influence you following your parent's death.

Cultural Dismissal

We Americans tend not to pay much attention to bereavement—or rather, we do our best to ignore it. Although the situation has changed somewhat during the past few decades, death and loss are still pretty much taboo subjects.

The American discomfort with bereavement affects all kinds of losses. Bereavement following a parent's death is not necessarily treated worse than the others. Yet one of the situations you face in grieving for a parent is the likelihood that some people will treat it as a non-event. As Marcia Lattanzi of the Boulder County (Colorado) Hospice puts it, "People sort of react to you as if, 'Oh, it was just your parent?' There's not much credence given to the death of one's parent as being a major event if one already has a family of one's own."

These cultural attitudes may complicate your feelings during the grief process. You may feel pressure from other people. You may start to consider your own emotions inappropriate or excessive. You may even question your basic sanity. After all, if a parent's death is no big deal, then why are you upset?

The dilemma is slightly different for men and for women. Our culture provides more leeway to women than to men for expressing emotions. In this sense, women are likely to grieve more openly; men are more likely to keep their grief under the surface. Yet because men have more practice in thwarting their emotions, the cultural pressures that affect everyone may be even more disruptive for women than for men. Ultimately, the crux of the matter is that these pressures are unfortunate for all people suffering a loss.

Too many people, both male and female, have experienced what Mark Cernik did after his mother's death: "When I got back to Phoenix after the funeral, I was in a very bad situation in terms of any kind of emotional support. The first time I talked to my roommates about what had happened, it was fine; they were compassionate and understanding. A month later, when I broke down and cried, they were embarrassed. They just couldn't handle it. One guy even said to another one, 'I think he's falling apart.' I wasn't falling apart at all; I was finally allowing myself to experience three griefs—my mother's death, her cancer of eighteen years before, and my father's death. Far from falling apart, I was falling together. For the first time. But people couldn't handle it."

One of the best ways for dealing with this situation is to find at least one real ally who can accept the complexities of your bereavement. Although a close friend or relative is ideal, sometimes your habitual confidants may be almost *too* close. This seems especially likely with a spouse or sibling, who may be too emotionally involved in his or her grief to understand your own. A friend who has also experienced loss—perhaps even the loss of a parent—seems more promising. Catherine K., who is forty-seven, lost her eighty-three-year-old father two years ago. One of the things that got her through the years of her father's illness and its aftermath was a thoughtful, kind friend. "I had two really close friends—one especially close," she says. "We have all sorts of stories about sitting around town in restaurants, drinking or eating breakfast, and talking about our parents' struggles—with literally both of us sitting there with tears streaming down our faces. It was just remarkable what she did for me."

Women have the advantage here. As a rule, men have fewer friends than women do with whom they can discuss emotional issues. Most of the men who told me of experiencing intense grief reactions mentioned their wife as the person who was most supportive. Other men found their sisters to be especially helpful. Unfortunately, few men described their brothers or male friends as sensitive toward their situations—or even interested in them. Quite the contrary, friends often seemed at a loss over how to deal with a man's bereavement. But there are alternatives. Two of them—often overlooked—are uncles and aunts. They are close enough to understand why your parents' deaths affect you, yet they're likely to have more perspective on the situation than you do.

In the final analysis, what matters most is that you remember the legitimacy of your emotions. You have every right to feel what you feel. You have the right to take your time grieving the death of your parent. Although you may have to take special pains to maintain your privacy during the grief process, you shouldn't deny the emotions themselves.

Memories

The death of someone you love breaks a kind of dam within the mind, and almost at once—whether you wish it or not—there is a flood of memories. Images, incidents, bits of conversation, shapeless feelings, and sometimes even hallucinations rush forth. If the relationship was hostile or uneasy, then the memories are almost certain to be turbulent.

But even if the relationship was happy, the sheer abundance and intensity of memories may seem overwhelming.

In the aftermath of a frightening crisis, you may also find that the events you witnessed—your parent's helplessness, frustration, and pain—now haunts you. You may worry that the experience of watching your parent suffer and die will displace your memories of the good times shared in the past. These worries are common, normal, and understandable. After all, you knew your parents longer than you have known anyone else; you probably recall their presence in your life from at least the age of four or five; and many of those recollections matter to you. It's frightening to think that recent events might end up more vivid than the long happy years preceding.

Some people feel a particularly intense sadness or revulsion at the memory of their parent's illness; for others, the harshest memory is of the death itself. Rod C.'s reaction is characteristic of what follows a sudden loss. Rod discovered his father's body one evening. (He is twenty-nine; his fifty-eight-year-old father died when Rod was twenty-eight.) Since then, the image of what he saw has plagued him: "I can no longer sleep nights. I keep envisioning my father dead in the living-room chair as I found him when I arrived that night." Jacqueline E.'s worries are more typical of what follows a parent's long illness. At the age of forty, Jacqueline lost both her seventy-seven-year-old father and her seventy-eight-year-old mother. "It will take a long time to heal the sore places—the memory of their suffering and struggle, the regret for mistakes and omissions," she says. To make matters worse, "It is hard to recall the good times together because the intense experience of their illness is so recent and vivid right now."

If you share either Jacqueline's or Rod's experiences, or if you've gone through a similar ordeal, you can rest assured that the painful recollections will ease. The vividness of your parent's suffering will dim; the images of dying and death will fade. This isn't to say that you will entirely forget what your parents went through. Loving your parents, you simply may not be able to watch them suffer and then be rid of the experience forever. But the intense, ugly memories that often linger following a death will diminish both in intensity and in frequency. More important, your earlier sense of your parents, your sense of them as vibrant and capable and happy, will return. Your recollections of good times and loving relationships are ultimately more powerful than the hardships that ended them.

Holidays and Anniversaries

Following your parent's death, you may also experience some difficulty during holidays and anniversaries. Dr. Raphael states that "The anniversary of a death or other anniversaries associated with it may result in reawakened bereavement." After all, holidays and anniversaries are times of intense emotion even under the best of circumstances; grief will intensify your reactions.

Strong feelings at a particular time of year seem all the more likely if you consider how much you associate certain holidays with your family. For most Christian families, Christmas provides the strongest images of family celebration and sharing. Passover, Chanukkah, and the High Holidays evoke similar feelings for Jews. Whether or not the festivities you recall were entirely as joyous as they now seem is beside the point; even the rough spots are emotionally charged. Thanksgiving, Mother's Day, Father's Day, your parents' birthdays, and the anniversaries of your parents' deaths can also affect you with special feelings. Which particular days affect you depends on family tradition, on your willingness to acknowledge your own feelings, and on other individual matters.

Mark Cernik has had to deal with conflicting emotions about the Christmas season because his father died at that time of year. "My father died at the age of fifty-three, of a heart attack, a week before Christmas," Mark says. "The funeral was on December twenty-second. I remember everything being bleak and black and cloudy and gray. Then everyone celebrated Christmas, and I just shut down completely. I just couldn't deal with it. For years after that, I couldn't deal with Christmas. I'd go through the motions. But I hated Christmas, I hated Christmas decorations, I hated Christmas carols—everything about it." Mark's feelings are not at all unusual for people who suffer a loss at that time of year. And almost any other holiday will absorb your feelings about your parent's death if the death occurs close to that time.

Even when a special occasion does not coincide with your parent's death, however, it can elicit strong emotions. For instance, Agnes U., who is fifty-eight (she was thirty-three when her father died at fifty-eight), finds that "Key times are still hard—births and special events in my life or my children's lives." Janice M., thirty-five (thirty-three when her fifty-seven-year-old mother died), feels that it was most difficult to get through the "firsts": "the first Christmas, the first Mother's Day, and so forth." Mother's Day and Father's Day are occasions that many people find difficult. Your parent's birthday may also bring up unexpectedly strong feelings after the death.

Your own birthday may do so as well. Louis W. found that "One of the hardest times was my own birthday. It was so difficult to deal with that day. I knew it would be. My wife had a great idea—which was to go out to the racetrack. I get totally absorbed at the racetrack. So we went, and it was fine. Later that evening, we went out to dinner; and when we came back, we were sitting out on the porch. The mail had come. There was a birthday card for me from my mother's best friend. And suddenly I just felt overwhelmed." This kind of reaction may seem surprising, but it makes sense. Your birthday—the actual day of your birth—was the start of your relationships with your parents; the anniversaries after that were celebrations of your existence and of your family's love for you; the whole occasion is emotionally charged. Many people's thoughts return to their parents during a birthday.

How to deal with your emotions at such times is a matter of individual preference. Some people prefer to acknowledge their recollections, others to ignore them. Either response is understandable. It's good to remember, however, that the intensity of recollection is often greatest during the first few years following a parent's death. You needn't worry that you will be awash in emotion during each holiday for the rest of your life. So you can indulge your memories without concern for becoming preoccupied. Some families even make a remembrance of the parent part of their celebration. For instance, Mark Cernik and his sister have a special routine when they visit each other: "Every time I go to see her, we drink a toast to Mother. Which is our little way of acknowledging that we haven't forgotten her even in death, and that her memory is still very much alive. And then we move on."

Ways of Dealing with Emotions and Memories

What else can you do to make the grief process easier? Although nothing will dispose of your grief all at once or take away all the pain, there are a number of ways to help yourself progress toward adjustment.

Diaries and Tape Recorders

To "get a handle" on your experiences, you might consider keeping a diary. Writing in a diary can serve any of several purposes: recording your thoughts, venting emotions, or reminiscing about your past. Perhaps it could serve one purpose initially and others later. For instance, you might start by expressing emotions about your parent's death, and later list some of the events that you found difficult during the illness. Still later, you might write about what had been satisfying about your relationship with your parent despite the hard times you went through recently. A diary can help you understand your thoughts and feelings about often confusing experiences. You may not know entirely why you're writing about something right at the moment, but putting your observations on paper may provide a chance for insights at a later date.

A few thoughts about keeping a diary:

- Don't worry about telling an organized or even a coherent story. Just start somewhere and go.
- Don't try to be "literary." You're not writing the Great American Novel—just putting your thoughts to paper.
- The diary is your private record. Find a quiet time and place to write, and let your family know that you need this time and solitude.

Another device for coming to terms with your experiences is the tape recorder. Although talking with a friend or relative about your parents may be preferable in many respects, talking into a tape recorder has its own advantages. It allows a free, uncensored form of reminiscing. You can say whatever is on your mind without worrying about a listener's reactions. As with a diary, you can express feelings that you might find too sensitive under other circumstances, and you can keep a record of events that may still be too confusing to understand.

A few suggestions:

- As when keeping a diary, don't worry about telling a coherent story. Feel free to ramble and jump around from the past to the present, and from one place to another. Let the ease of talking open up your memory.
- Feel free to express your emotions even if what you're talking about upsets you. Tape recorders are wonderfully

tolerant machines; they will listen to whatever you say without impatience or embarrassment.
- What you're doing is for your use only. Find a quiet time and place to speak into the machine, and let your family know that you need some privacy for this purpose.

Later, you may want to use the tape recorder for a different purpose: telling stories about your parents, your childhood, and times past. This method serves less to vent emotions than to record events for the future—not only for your own use, but even for sharing family tales, anecdotes, and reflections at a later time. Recording stories in this way can be especially important if your own children never knew your parents. They may not be interested now, but they might be when they grow older. In short, the tape recorder can provide a means for preserving family history.

Making Peace with Your Parents

One of the regrets that adults often express following parental loss is their inability to work through old conflicts with their parents. There is almost always unfinished business in a relationship. When parents die, the chance to resolve conflicts and soothe old hurts is gone forever.

Or is it? The fact of the matter is that the chance is never completely gone. Even following a parent's death, it's possible to settle unfinished business. The reason is that many of your reactions to your parents aren't just reactions to your actual mother and father, but are at least partly reactions to a kind of internal image of them. All of us acquire these internal parents as we grow up. Although your parent's death makes it impossible to deal with the person who was once alive, you can still approach those internal parents and resolve many or all of the conflicts that you feel toward them.

Harold Bloomfield, an American psychiatrist, has developed a program to help adults deal with parent-child conflicts. Dr. Bloomfield uses this program in his own private practice in California, but he has also published a book, *Making Peace with Your Parents*, that helps adults use the same program themselves. Dr. Bloomfield states that this program "is not an overnight cure-all." It is, however, a series of exercises that can be useful in resolving old resentments, disengaging from unrealistic expectations, and avoiding destructive relationships. Dr. Bloomfield believes that these exercises can be effective whether your parents are alive or have died. In fact, his book includes a chapter, complete with exercises, devoted entirely to helping adults cope with parental loss.

Although not suitable for everyone, Dr. Bloomfield's program is one of the most accessible ways of resolving leftover conflicts with your parents after their deaths. See Appendix C for further information.

Psychotherapy

Depending on how you feel following your parent's death, you may also want to consider the possibility of counseling or psychotherapy. Emotions or practical circumstances during the grief process are often complex enough that even the most insightful, capable person could benefit from another perspective. Psychiatrists, psychologists, social workers, and other mental health professionals are trained precisely for this purpose. Some of them are even specialists in working with the bereaved.

There are many options available to people who want counseling or psychotherapy. Because of their number and variety, however, we will cover the subject fully in Chapter Nine.

Health Issues and Bereavement

In the aftermath of a parent's death, the stresses may not be just emotional, but physical as well. Kate S., fifty-one (she was thirty-five when her father died at sixty-two), summed up her situation after her father's long illness: "I didn't realize how physically and mentally exhausted I'd become." Mark Cernik's reaction was brief but intense: "I was absolutely exhausted and numb when I got back to Phoenix. I left immediately after that to visit a friend in Louisiana. And I slept twelve hours a day for seven days. I just couldn't cope with what had happened anymore; I just shut down. I didn't want to talk about it, I didn't want to think about it— I just wanted to sleep." Many other adult daughters and sons find their health affected during or after a parent's illness.

Health would be a minor problem if bereavement were the brief and tidy matter that many people still expect it to be. But because grief often lasts a long time, you can damage your health if you don't understand the stresses it can create. The risk is especially high if caring for your parent during a long illness has already exhausted you.

Sleep

Probably the first part of your routine to suffer is sleep. Medical emergencies, late-night consultations with friends and relatives, and other disruptions of your normal sleeping pattern can take their toll during a parent's illness. Depression following the death often makes matters worse. When depressed, many people suffer insomnia—either as difficulty in falling asleep or in staying asleep. If you're having these problems, try to compensate for sleep loss if you can. Almost any arrangement you can make to avoid exhaustion will be worth the effort. It may be tempting to proceed with your usual activities at full speed, but you will eventually suffer the effects.

Diet

Eating right can be surprisingly difficult during the grief process. Depression suppresses the appetite; even *feeling* hungry may be difficult. Fixing a meal or going out may not seem worth the trouble. Yet bad nutrition can intensify your fatigue and depression; it can also lower your resistance and leave you vulnerable to illness. Very few crises justify damaging your health and state of mind through malnutrition. Keeping yourself properly fed can make a great difference not only in your physical well-being but in your outlook as well.

Medical Care

Compared to your parent's illness, your own aches and pains seem trivial. Perhaps they are. But perhaps not. Fatigue alone can cause serious health problems or aggravate those already existing. According to current research, emotional stress can demonstrably affect people's health. Since fatigue and stress are common during the grief process, you are probably vulnerable to illness. This is not to say that you will contract some sort of horrendous malady. But following a major loss, you should be especially attentive to your health. If you have reasons to question your level of well-being, get a checkup. Stress-induced and stress-aggravated illnesses are just as real as any others. And if your physician gives you a clean bill of health—which is likely—then the good news will take that much worry off your mind.

Alcohol and Drugs

Because bereavement can alter your daily routines, disrupt your sleep, affect your appetite, and intensify your emotions, you may feel a need to ease the pressure by increasing consumption of alcohol or drugs. This inclination is a common response. Certain mourning customs—the wake, for instance—actually encourage heavy drinking. But if you find that you ease the pressures of bereavement by drinking or taking drugs, you should be careful of the consequences. Use of alcohol or drugs to ease your grief can complicate rather than simplify your adjustment. One reason is that you may become more reliant on drinking or drug-taking than you would be at other times. Another reason is that alcohol and drug abuse will probably disrupt your appetite and sleep pattern, thus increasing the likelihood of poor nutrition, fatigue, and their consequences.

If you feel that your consumption of alcohol or drugs has increased during bereavement, you should consult a qualified counselor for advice. Drugs and alcohol can't lead you through the grief process. Overuse can only obstruct your way back to a normal life.

Problematic Bereavement

You will probably work your way through the grief process without major difficulties. As is true for other challenging experiences, however, it's worthwhile to know the danger signals. They are what we discussed regarding your surviving parent's bereavement—and they apply to you as well:

- protracted inability to believe that your parent has really died;
- protracted social isolation following the death;
- inability to care for yourself;
- reliance on alcohol or drugs to relieve a sense of anguish, loneliness, anger, or other emotions;
- extensive changing of plans or making of decisions according to what your parent would have preferred, rather than according to your own preferences;
- great effort to *avoid* thinking of the parent;
- substantial weight gain, weight loss, or marked deterioration of health;
- suicidal thoughts or gestures, or attempted suicide;
- inability to "get on" with life, to invest energy in living.

If you feel that you are experiencing problems in any of these ways, you should contact a qualified counselor for help. What you are going through is probably not a long-term problem, but you will be better off discussing the issues than ignoring them.

Emotional Leeway

Looking after yourself during bereavement is more than just a matter of staying rested, fed, and healthy, but treating yourself well in these ways is a necessary start. In addition, you should give yourself some emotional leeway. Don't expect too much too soon. Bereavement is hard work—and often long work as well. As Marcia Lattanzi puts it, "Be gentle with yourself." Wendy Foster-Evans elaborates on this theme: "People often think that they should get better quickly, and if they're still feeling bad two months later, there's something wrong with them. Well, that's not true. People need to go at their own pace and in their own way."

The most important thing for you to keep in mind is that you will almost certainly go through the grief process without harm. "Most people deal pretty well with the loss of a parent," according to Dr. Weiss, "and most often recover uneventfully." The human organism can not only withstand the stresses of loss but often prevails over them as well.

The Potential for Positive Change

One of the most unusual aspects of parental loss is, in fact, the potential for positive change in its aftermath. Other forms of loss bring with them a potential for change as well; loss of almost any sort can jolt, frighten, or inspire you into altering your beliefs, feelings, or activities. In this regard, loss of a parent isn't fundamentally different from other losses. During our interview, Dr. Parkes stated, "I happen to believe that most major changes that people face in their lives are both threats to health and also opportunities for growth. The more I study bereavement, the more convinced

I become that transcending grief—coming through the process in a healthy way—is a growth-promoting experience, however painful it may be, in the vast majority of people who go through it."

Moreover, evidence suggests that loss of a parent brings with it an unusually great potential for personal change. There are two explanations for this potential. One, as we have discussed already, is that a parent's death, no matter how sad, often seems less unjust than other deaths. Obviously the individual circumstances of your parent's death will make a difference in how you feel. But generally speaking, parental loss is less likely to wrench your life apart with the sheer sense of injustice that other losses create. As a result, you will probably feel less cheated or betrayed than you would following other losses. The other explanation is that during and after a parent's illness and death, you may take on new roles, acquire new interests, enter new phases of your career, develop new attitudes, or take on new responsibilities that you might not have otherwise. This experience can foster new confidence and competence. As a recent Institute of Medicine report on bereavement states, "The death [of a parent] is often experienced as a 'developmental push,' propelling the adult into the next stage of life."

Such changes do not, of course, mean that all problems are solved, all uncertainties clarified, all worries relieved. Neither does it mean that if you experience positive changes, you won't also deeply regret your parents' deaths and grieve their absence from your life. But the potential for change is there; many people experience it; and the benefits are often long-lasting.

Here is a sampling of what men and women have said about how their parents' deaths changed their lives:

> "My parents' deaths made me grow up. I was always protected by my parents. Suddenly I was in charge."

—Claudia V., forty-two (thirty-seven when her mother died at sixty-eight; forty when her father died at sixty-eight)

"It changed my position to being part of the older generation. I feel a greater sense of responsibility for keeping the family intact."
—Audrey D., thirty-nine (twenty-nine when her mother died at sixty-seven; thirty-seven when her father died at seventy-two)

"I grew and emerged a much stronger, self-reliant, capable person, a better role model for my daughters, and a better helpmate for my husband."
—Joyce E., forty-six (thirty-five when her father died at seventy; thirty-six when her mother died at sixty-eight)

"I believe my father's death began a period of maturity that I would not have achieved otherwise. Much of what he was, *I* was now expected to be. There was no more 'passing the buck.'"
—Patricia L., thirty-six (twenty-seven when her father died at sixty-two; twenty-nine when her mother died at sixty-one)

Does this mean that you should necessarily find your parent's death a transforming experience? Not at all. Some people do; some don't. Many people find parental loss vastly less than a positive change in their lives. Sometimes it's only negative—a bleak stretch, an ordeal, a time to get through. Unalloyed difficulty of this sort doesn't mean that something is wrong with you. It means simply that the circumstances of your relationships, or of the particular task you faced, have been too demanding or exhausting to allow for more positive side effects. Unfortunately, the range of situations that sons and daughters face when parents die includes some that lack any substantial consolations. It's hard to feel transformed by twenty years' effort of nursing a sick parent. If you have run this kind of gauntlet, you should feel proud enough simply to have endured.

If, however, you feel some sort of creative change following your parent's death, there's nothing wrong with your attitude. It *is* a relief to finish with heavy responsibilities. It *is* a delight to proceed with your own life again. It *is* a source of pride to learn from your parents, to carry on a long and complex relationship with them—complete with normal ups and downs—and to accompany them into the final stage of their lives. There's no reason why you shouldn't feel a kind of release when even a good relationship ends.

You're now free to proceed. Whatever duties may have burdened you, whatever roles may have confined you, whatever expectations may have restrained you—you can now move on in whatever direction you want your life to take.

NINE

COUNSELING, THERAPY, AND SUPPORT GROUPS

But now we come to a stumbling block. If, as it seems, the grief process is usually normal—even *creative*—then what should we do when it seems intolerably painful, complex, messy, and wearisome? How should we deal with it when we couldn't care less about growth or change, and we just want life to be comfortable again? Should we just muddle through? Should we pull ourselves up by our bootstraps? Or are there other alternatives?

As with other aspects of bereavement and grief, the answer is extremely personal. Some people find solace in work or play; others seek out companions; still others withdraw for a while. Each of these responses to loss makes sense to some degree. We *need* activity. We *need* companionship. We *need* solitude. Ultimately, we must return to the outside world and all its complex ways of involving us. Yet each of these responses also contains an element of risk. It's not a matter of the basic impulse—"moving along," "getting on with life," and so forth. Rather, it's a matter of timing. Sometimes dealing with the grief process is easier if we move inward before we move out into the world again.

There are some important options to consider in this regard. Some people, on experiencing the confusion that often follows a death, seek counseling or therapy to help them deal with their situations. The options are growing more and more numerous and accessible. Americans look to professional guidance for family conflicts, job problems, and all sorts of other crises, so why shouldn't the death of a parent receive the same concern? Unfortunately, some people dismiss the possibility out of hand. Perhaps you've done this yourself. "I knew Mother (or Father) was going to die," you say. "It's not as if the death took me by surprise." Or else you simply decide, "I'll get over it." These statements are true—but at least partly irrelevant. Like most people, you will come to terms with your loss. But there's no reason why you have to do so alone. Talking with a trained counselor or therapist can make the grief process smoother, easier, and a lot less lonely.

The Whys and Wherefores of Therapy

What are typical experiences during therapy after a parent's death? That's a difficult question to answer. Therapy is such a personal experience that it's questionable if anyone's experience of it is "typical." On the other hand, my interviews with people who have sought therapy following parental loss suggest that most of them do so with fairly similar problems in mind. There seem to be four clusters of issues here. (The question of results is another matter—one that we'll consider shortly.)

One cluster is what we might call **emotional issues.** As we have already noted, many people feel depressed, lonely, angry, guilty, and confused in the aftermath of a major loss. These are normal emotions, but their intensity sometimes exceeds normal levels of tolerance.

A second cluster comes out of the first: **physical issues.** These are the sleep disturbances, eating problems, fatigue, and illness that can affect you at times of great emotional stress. Some people tend to label these problems "psychosomatic" and to dismiss them as inconsequential. However, difficulties like insomnia, loss of appetite or overeating, chronic fatigue, and even ailments like high blood pressure and ulcers are genuine risks as a consequence of stress during the grief process.

The third cluster includes **family, marital, and job issues.** Some of these may result from the other issues. For instance, depression or fatigue may complicate your relationships with the people around you. On the other hand, some of the conflicts may be considerable in their own right—whether preexisting (such as a shaky marriage) or aggravated by grief.

The fourth cluster of issues is subtle but also important—what we might call **existential issues.** Death and grief frequently reveal new meanings to our lives, or else cast old meanings into doubt. In the aftermath of a parent's death, you may start wondering what went on in your past to account for who you are, or you may wish to change your behavior in the future.

There may be other reasons for seeking therapy, but most people who seek therapy during bereavement are dealing with at least one of these issues, and probably with more than one. Simply determining where one issue leaves off and another starts is often difficult. Such complicated aspects of our feelings often become entangled. Following a parent's death, for instance, most people feel depressed—but what causes the depression? Is it a sense of loss? Loneliness? Is it perhaps a side effect of unexpressed anger? If so, anger toward whom? Toward brothers and sisters? Toward other relatives? Maybe toward the parent? And what are the results of all these emotions? Conflicts with others? Withdrawal from them? Job problems? In trying to make sense of all these feelings, it's no wonder that we end up still more exhausted and confused.

Wanting to make sense of such complex issues is sufficient reason for therapy. But there's something else to consider: sometimes there is no clear "reason" at all. There is no single event or conflict or feeling that makes it seem necessary. In fact, many people—whether before or after a parent's death—don't pinpoint a particular issue and decide to seek help for it. There is simply a sense that something is out of kilter.

The crises are over now, you tell yourself. You did what you could. There's nothing more to do now but return to the life you've been living. But then you add: not yet. Not entirely. You're too tired, too confused. It's nothing in particular. Something is wrong, but you don't know what it is.

Kinds of Therapy

So you decide to see a therapist. Now what? Of course, therapists use many different techniques, some of them more appropriate for certain situations than others; but in general, therapy during the grief process serves much the same purposes as it does under other circumstances. It allows you to express emotions. It provides a place for clarifying problems and exploring possible solutions. It encourages careful decision-making. And it builds confidence between you and the therapist in ways that help you to undertake these other tasks together. Early on, therapy may focus on the bewilderment, anger, and depression that you feel right after a parent's death. Later, it may shift to examine other matters—what took place in the past or what's going to happen in the future.

One-to-One Therapy

Therapists have many methods for helping their clients deal with bereavement. The following comments are not indicative of how *all* therapists work with the bereaved; however, my interview with William K. Dixon, a Gestalt therapist, revealed techniques that are characteristic of many kinds of one-to-one therapy.

"Within Gestalt therapy there's an emphasis on experiencing rather than talking or analyzing," Dr. Dixon explains. "What I often invite people to do when they want some help working through grief is to imagine—if they're willing—the person they have lost. Sometimes it's helpful to do that even as if at the funeral or at the deathbed. For some people, it's more helpful to imagine a time shortly before death, so that they can have that sense of expressing something to the person while that person would still have been able to listen.

"What I ask them to do, then, is to begin expressing some things with that person: some things which they particularly appreciate; some things which they feel bad about; some things which made them feel fortunate; and even some things which make them resentful. People often feel that when someone dies, they have no right to be angry with the person; they think they're required to forgive everything. But a lot of times, that forgiveness can't happen until the person gets in touch with the resentments which have lingered. And so I try to find an opportunity for the person to express those resentments as directly as possible.

"Something else which also seems to be helpful is asking the client to imagine what they are taking with them from that relationship. It might be particular memories; it might be a skill that they learned from that person; it might be a certain attitude or feeling which they want to continue to have. Conversely, I ask them what they want to leave behind or bury with that person. Sometimes that's where some of the forgiveness happens. 'I'm leaving behind those memories of painful times we had,' for instance. Or, 'I'm leaving behind the resentment I feel for the times you scolded me.' And they express that.

"Finally, I ask the person to say goodbye. Often, a person is not really willing to say goodbye. Certainly a person can say those words; but in terms of being able to say goodbye and leave the person behind—so that they have psychologically buried the one they've lost—that may be another matter. If they resist that, then I acknowledge it. And I check with them if that might be an indication that some feelings are left unexpressed, and that psychologically this is the reason why it's hard to let go. Generally, people are able to recognize that there's still some unfinished business; there are some strong feelings; and it's too soon to really imagine letting go. In that case, we generally agree to come back to that. It usually seems appropriate to the client.

"This process might take place over one session that we'll use for this purpose, or it might take place over a period of several months. There is a lot of individual difference, of course. Sometimes I encourage a person to deal with just part of the grief. At a later time, when the person seems to be readier, then we can proceed. People generally have a good sense of their own timing."

Bereavement Groups

One-to-one therapy—whether with a psychiatrist, psychologist, social worker, or other counselor—is often helpful during the grief process. But what if individual therapy isn't feasible? What if it isn't even preferable? What are the alternatives?

One possibility is what has come to be called the bereavement group. (Organizers and members also call them grief workshops, bereavement seminars, mourning clinics, and so forth.) Despite their numerous titles, these groups all provide some form of group therapy or "consciousness-raising." Some stress self-help and are a form of peer counseling. Others use a trained "facilitator"—sometimes a volunteer, sometimes a paid staff member—to provide guidance in ways that might otherwise be lacking. Either way, the members meet to discuss their problems; they listen to each other and perhaps offer suggestions or encouragement; but they do not perform therapy in a traditional sense. The emphasis most often is on mutual supportiveness among people facing similar predicaments.

Omega, mentioned earlier, is located in Somerville, Massachusetts, near Boston. Omega offers emotional support and information for the ill, the dying, their families, and the bereaved. Omega provides several distinct services, but perhaps the most innovative are its bereavement groups. These include two specifically for widows and widowers, one for persons who have lost someone through suicide, and one for anyone else in the aftermath of a friend's or a family member's death. Many of the participants in this third group are adults who have lost a parent.

Evelyn Gladu, Omega's director, explains how this organization helps its clients: "All we do is to create a safe place for people to express whatever they feel during their grief. Different people use the group in different ways. We set it up so that people can respond in a way that will be helpful to them." Ms. Gladu has found that the most helpful structure is groups (of varying sizes) meeting with trained facilitators. Sessions last several hours twice a month at regularly scheduled times. The format itself is flexible. According to Ms. Gladu, "The facilitator opens each meeting with a prefacing statement about the nature of the group. Then it's entirely up to members to share concerns, issues, and feelings. People quickly sense that the group is a safe place to express whatever they wish, because they are among others who are also grieving. As facilitators, we never have the problem of 'bringing people out.' People respond to each other."

What happens to people during an Omega group? In part, the process is cathartic. The bereavement group does in fact seem to provide the "safe place" that Ms. Gladu and her co-workers want it to be, and many participants in the group find themselves able to feel and express what has seemed embarrassing or even forbidden elsewhere. Crying, laughter, anger, and other emotions are all permissible. This in itself frequently allows participants an intense feeling of relief. There is also a social dimension to the experience. Group members each discover that the others have gone through experiences similar to their own, and at least *some* people understand what bereavement is like. This affirms the participants' sense that their emotions are not only normal but perhaps even necessary for getting through a difficult phase of life. Ms. Gladu suggests that the result of these insights on the group and its members is often a stronger, more confident grasp of the meaning of loss.

"What is especially satisfying," Ms. Gladu says, "is that there is a lot of movement. Sometimes people themselves don't see it until coming to the other side of the process. They feel better. They've been in pain for months, but *we* see that things have changed. The pain, if it continues throughout the sessions, is often pain over different issues from what it was before. They're moving. Sometimes we point that out to people."

There are many groups like Omega now, and others are taking shape each year, for the concept appeals to some people more than traditional therapies do. The spread of bereavement groups seems partly a side effect of the hospice movement. Just as hospice care often meets special needs of the dying, these groups meet special needs of the bereaved. Various hospice organizations have, in fact, set up their own bereavement programs. For instance, Cabrini Hospice in New York City runs a group for relatives of former patients; the Hospice of Marin, located in San Rafael, California, maintains a variety of bereavement services, including groups; the Hospice of Boulder County, in Colorado, has also organized a group as part of its program. These groups differ from each other in various ways, but their basic purposes are similar. And in all probability, they are only the start of a more widespread development.

What should you do if you want to join a bereavement group but can't find one? Try calling the city or state department of social services for information. If that doesn't help, call the social services department of your local hospital. Some hospitals are now setting up their own hospices, which may include bereavement programs; other hospitals may be able to refer you to a local hospice. Ministers, rabbis, and priests may also know of available resources within your community. However, if all these various avenues lead nowhere, you can try two national information centers designed specifically to help out at such times. One is the National Hospice Organization. The other is the National Self-Help Clearinghouse. (See Appendix B for details.)

This brings us to one last consideration. Is a bereavement group what you want? Is it, for that matter, what you need?

Without question, the concept of the bereavement group has tremendous potential. The specific groups I've visited are impressive. Their staff members are thoughtful, perceptive, and warm. I don't sense any of the hucksterism that permeates some other kinds of therapy. In addition, bereavement groups often serve a function beyond that of one-to-one therapy—specifically, to provide a sense of common experience and support among people going through substantial changes in their lives. These are highly valuable attributes. And under some circumstances, bereavement groups may end up not just the best option, but the only one at all.

Yet you should still choose carefully. Not every person should enter therapy, and not every method or therapist is suitable for each person. Many factors influence whether a bereavement group is appropriate. Consequently, some therapists have strong misgivings about the spread of bereavement groups. Anne Rosberger, a therapist who works with both individual clients and groups at the Bereavement and Loss Center in New York, warns against the assumption that groups are always suitable. "There's an attitude," she states, "that being in a group is the panacea. I don't believe it. There are some very good things that come out of groups, and there are some terribly damaging things." Specifically, Ms. Rosberger expresses concern that bereavement groups may not allow for sufficiently individualized attention to participants. Moreover, the dynamics of group interaction are so unpredictable that monitoring them requires a highly skilled leader. Ms. Rosberger therefore believes that the usefulness of a group depends on a client's needs, the therapist's abilities, and the particular "match" between them.

So how can you know what's appropriate for you? Perhaps the first course of action is to ask the opinion of a trusted physician, member of the clergy, or friend. Many cities also have psychiatric referral services. These services can provide at least a start in finding appropriate therapy.

Ultimately, you will have to trust your own hunches. You are the only one who can make sense of your experiences—including the experience of grief. This doesn't mean that you have to figure everything out yourself, but you have a right to choose the guides along the way. This may mean picking someone to coax you gently, or perhaps someone to challenge you. It may mean a single mentor or a group of insightful peers. It's hard to know what's preferable. Perhaps you never know for sure; you simply have to choose carefully and see what happens.

What Therapy Does

Last, the crucial question: does therapy make a difference?

Of the people I interviewed or contacted through questionnaires, 42 out of 217 had sought therapy to help them deal with the experience. Thirty-two of those who had sought therapy felt that it had helped them with their bereavement. Of course the sense of what helped is extremely subjective.

Cynthia Sanderson initially went to a therapist to relieve a sense of internal pressure: "My major need was to talk to people about what had happened. I talked to my husband, but he knew the whole story; he'd lived through it. And I'd just keep saying the same things. He was very nice about listening, but I felt like I couldn't keep telling him. So going to a therapist was good, in that there was somebody to tell the whole story." After several months, however, Cynthia found that her therapy had shifted to another purpose. She was coming to terms not just with the deaths, but with her whole relationship with her parents. "The incredible discovery was that the process [of dealing with issues within the relationships] can go on even after they've died. The hardest thing has been to try and establish my own sense of myself without risking my attachment to them that I want to hold on to." For fifteen months, Cynthia worked through these issues with her therapist. She dropped out of therapy when she felt that these issues had adequately resolved.

Mark Cernik had a longer, more complex experience. Shortly after his mother died, he entered therapy. The initial months focused on his mother's illness and death, but Mark soon realized that there were other issues on his mind. "Once I got into therapy, I realized that I'd never really worked through my father's death, either, because I never really buried him." Mark's therapist guided him toward realizations about the earlier loss. "What I found was that while talking it out, talking about the experiences and experiencing them, certain ones would have an emotional impact. That was one of the freeing things. Because once I put words to it, it was as if it didn't have power over me. Whereas before, it had been an undifferentiated mass of anxiety, sadness, and fear." After about a year, Mark felt sufficiently relieved of his previous tensions that he finished therapy. "Given what I wanted to work through, things had been pretty much resolved. I'd check back with him about every six months—just for a little conversation. But it was my sense and his sense that we were really finished."

Here are briefer comments that other people have made about their experiences with therapy:

> Winnie C., thirty-eight: "During the first few years of grieving, my therapist simply remained a rock—the one solid thing I could count on in my life. Since then, I have been able to share almost all of my sadness and anger with her about the deaths."

> Carlota A., thirty-five: "I was in therapy, and that helped me deal with much of the ambivalence that I had, and with the residual childhood feelings."

> Janice M., thirty-five: "I saw a counselor, whose main work is in the area of death and dying, before my mother died. I found it to be a tremendous help. I was able, with her help, to separate my feelings, fears, anger, and grief—to try to cope with them one at a time."

> Jessie Y., forty-four: "Counseling made a tremendous difference for me. It was an opportunity to ventilate my anger, verbalize my fears, receive moral support and learn some assertiveness skills. The two years of weekly visits to a sensitive and caring counselor were well worth the investment in time, money, and emotional upheaval. Counseling was an extremely therapeutic experience for which I will always be grateful."

> Sari N., forty-four: "I did not allow myself to grieve—I was detached from many relationships. Therapy helped me understand my behavior and take risks for change."

What these and other experiences suggest is that therapy following a parent's death can help you deal with bereavement. In what ways it helps, and to what degree, varies from person to person. The specific reactions differ; the overall pattern, however, is fairly clear.

My own experience was in keeping with this pattern. I

entered therapy soon after my mother's death and continued with it for about ten months. I found that therapy made an emphatic difference in coming to terms not only with my mother's death but with my father's as well. (Although my father had died nine years before Mother did, that event remained unresolved in some ways.) The psychotherapy I went through following Mother's death was some of the hardest work I've ever done, but it was invaluable. I can't recall any comparable period of time in my adult life when I've learned so much about myself. In a number of ways, I came out of the experience greatly changed. I'm not at all implying that this therapy was some sort of miracle cure or transformation; on the contrary, much of what happened was exasperatingly uncertain, ambiguous, even contradictory. But it made a big difference.

The simplest way for me to explain is this: therapy made it easier to understand how I fit into my family, and how my family fit into the surrounding world. I suspect that sooner or later, I would have figured this out anyway. Therapy didn't make it possible, just easier. It was also much less lonely this way. Contemporary life provides us with precious few guides, and finding a good one—even for six or eight months—is a breakthrough. But speaking of guides may give the wrong impression. My therapist wasn't a guide in the sense of leading me somewhere; at least he didn't in any way that I could consciously follow. Instead, he let me blunder about until I found my own way.

Perhaps herein lies the real wisdom of the approach. It was difficult. At times, it was harrowing. But in the long run—and I mean a long run that is still under way—it has helped me to figure out who I am, and why.

Grief is only the beginning.

TEN

CONCLUSION: THE LETTER FROM BEYOND

A few days after my father died, I discovered a letter he had written to me just before he took ill. The letter was stamped and addressed and ready to mail, and it lay among some other papers on his desk. Writing that letter was probably one of the last things Codger had done. He simply had never gotten around to mailing it at the corner postbox.

I resisted opening that letter for a while. Somehow it seemed heavy, burdensome, almost dangerous, as if inevitably bringing more bad news to what we had already received. Whatever else, it reminded me once again of how abruptly Codger's life had been cut short. It seemed ominous—not just a letter, but The Letter. Other members of my family felt the same way about it. We made a mildly uncomfortable joke of the letter and nicknamed it The Letter from Beyond.

But soon my curiosity got the best of me. I opened the envelope and read the letter.

April 29, 1972

Dear Eddy—
    The snows of day-before-yesterday have all but gone. Late this afternoon there were only a few splotches of white still on the yard.

For some time now I have thought more or less idly about buying a beret. The last time I set out to look, I decided to buy a more or less standard hat, for the brim. I am now back to where I was before—convinced that for these days that are neither very bright nor especially wet, the beret is ideal. . . .

He related the story of his unsuccessful quest for a beret, then went on to discuss my previous letter, some possible plans I had suggested for the coming summer, and his current classes at the university. He closed with a few comments about my likely return to Denver.

How, when, and in what state (in regard to talking, for example) you should arrive here is no matter. Do it when and as it is best for you.

All our love,
Francis

Reading that letter, I was relieved. It was just a letter. There was nothing ominous or threatening about it. Although the circumstances were emotionally difficult, nothing in them prevented me from regarding this letter as simply a final communication from my dad. Codger and I had carried on a long correspondence, writing to each other several times a week during my college years and travels, extending to paper the conversation we carried on so elaborately in person. This letter was different from the others only because it was the last.

Yet I discovered that my relief was mixed with disappointment. Was this *all?* Wasn't there more to my dad's final days than looking for a beret and observing the aftermath of a snowstorm? The letter seemed insubstantial. Didn't he have any grand last words? Didn't he want to offer me some final advice? He hadn't known he was dying, of course, but *still*. . . . I found it hard to believe that someone as observant and thoughtful as he—a professional philosopher, yet—would exit chattering about a hat.

Perhaps, I decided, the letter wasn't just what it seemed. Perhaps it contained a secret message—not something that Codger had made intentionally obscure, but rather accidentally so, veiled by the workings of his unconscious mind. Perhaps the letter, properly read, revealed a private allegory.

For many years afterward, I've read and reread The Letter from Beyond. I've read it slowly, read it fast, read it literally and figuratively between the lines, read it in just about all ways except backwards. Never during all that time have I found symbols or messages or allegories. All I found was the letter. All I discovered there was my father's quest for a beret, his delight in the weather, his fascination with teaching, his curiosity about my activities and plans, his affection for me. The same has been true for his other letters. Likewise for my mother's—I've kept hers also. And likewise for my recollections of both my mother and dad. They went about their business, they worked and played, they ate and slept, they visited their friends, they watched TV and listened to music, they felt depressed at times and happy at other times, they wondered what it all meant. Both died younger than they should have. Both, despite their untimely deaths, lived full lives.

The Letter from Beyond never panned out as a private allegory, but it ended up serving other purposes. Along with my parents' other letters, a box of unsorted photographs, and various of their personal effects, The Letter from Beyond has remained one of the most evocative reminders of my life with them. It's not as if I spend a lot of time thinking about this letter. On the contrary, I've forgotten about it for entire years, I've lost it once or twice, and ordinarily I can't quite remember where I've stashed it. In a folder, in a box, in a closet somewhere . . . ? But the letter crops up now and then, either as the actual sheet of paper and the envelope, or as a recollection. And the letter, when I look at it or think of it, reminds me both of what I had in growing up with my parents and, too, what I lost when they died. In this sense, the letter is fundamentally a memento—my version of the proverbial photo on the mantelpiece. But it's a particular kind of memento. It doesn't just remind me of my parents; it also reminds me of where I am in relation to them, both in the ways that change and the ways that stay the same.

Fourteen years have now passed since my dad's death; five since my mother's. There's no question in my mind that I've come to terms with my parents' deaths, and in fact came to terms with them years ago. I've accepted what happened. I've accepted my parents' absence from my life. I feel little of the sadness and anger that I once did when I think of their illnesses. My mother's death is more recent, and her situation was ultimately more appalling, so my recollections of her have a stronger intensity. But for several years now, I've found my memories of both parents less likely to linger on their struggles and deaths, and more likely to focus on the years before—on my upbringing with them in Denver, on the years we lived in Peru and Mexico, on my adolescent upheavals, on the closeness my dad and I reached during the 1960s and early 1970s, on the later closeness between my mother and me.

In keeping with the changes in my sense of what happened over the years, The Letter from Beyond, like virtually everything else that reminds me of my parents, now reminds me of these two remarkable people and not of what befell them at the end of their lives. The letter reminds me of events separated both in time and in space from what my dad wrote about in 1972.

I am twenty-six. My mother, sitting with me on the balcony of a house she rented for a while in Mexico, recounts the story of some local boys who sold her an owl they had caught.

I am twenty. My father strides next to me on one of our walks and listens intently as I tell him about a book I am writing.

I am sixteen. My mother points out a web of shadow cast by a hanging fern onto the wall.

I am eleven. My father, exhaling vapor into the winter air, pulls me through the snow on a sled.

I am six. My mother shows me a secret bird's nest in a juniper to ease my guilt over some robin's eggs I had stolen from another tree.

I am four. I have awakened, crying. My father carries me into the dark kitchen. Now we are both silent. There is no illumination except for diagonals of light cast to the floor from a corner streetlamp.

What does a parent's death mean? Ultimately, despite my own experiences, despite my research, despite my thinking over the whole matter for years, I have to admit that I don't know. Not really; not fully. How can I grasp the fact that my parents made my life possible? How can I perceive the depth of their influence on my childhood? How can I calculate the effects of what they gave me, showed me, taught me over a period of twenty or thirty years? Until I can answer these questions, I have to doubt how deeply and broadly I understand their deaths.

But I can tell you this: some years ago—shortly after my mother's death—I finally understood The Letter from Beyond. My dad had pulled the old purloined-letter trick. (Remember the Edgar Allan Poe story in which someone hides a letter by leaving it in plain view, right on the mantelpiece?) There was no hidden symbol. No secret message. No private allegory. The Letter from Beyond wasn't a letter from Beyond. It was from Here.

We shared the lives we lived; shared delight, uncertainty, amusement, and occasional frustration toward each other; shared insight and misunderstanding; shared time together and, too, shared the understanding that there would be time apart.

We shared what we had the sense to share. It was a lot. And it was good.

APPENDICES

APPENDIX A

SUMMARY OF RESEARCH METHODS

In researching *When Parents Die*, I used four different methods. Two involved acquiring information directly from adults who have lost one or both parents; two involved borrowing the insights, observations, and recommendations of mental health professionals who work with the bereaved either as researchers or clinicians.

My earliest research method—and to some degree the most satisfying—emphasized long, in-person interviews with persons who have experienced the loss of a parent. I say "satisfying" because I found that this method provided the fullest portrait of what a parent's death means to individual men and women, and, in addition, the best sense of how these individuals' experiences differ. Moreover, as a novelist and journalist, I found that this method offered the subtlest portrait as well. It's a matter of professional preference. Empirical psychologists would disagree with me, but I find people's stories about their experiences most interesting precisely when most unquantifiable. There are, of course, drawbacks to this method. But they are the drawbacks that I personally prefer to those present in more structured forms of research.

Between the summer of 1982 and the winter of 1984, I interviewed thirty-four people, either in person or by phone.

These interviews lasted from forty-five minutes to seven hours. The persons I interviewed were primarily friends, relatives, and their friends and relatives, plus acquaintances met during the course of my work on the book. Of these thirty-four people, twenty-seven were women and seven were men. Their ages ranged from thirty to sixty-five.

Ideally, I would have liked to make interviews of this sort the basis for all my research. Nothing ultimately served my purposes better than lengthy, detailed conversations on a wide variety of issues. I realized during early 1983, however, that the time and expense involved in this method would restrict the range of my research if limited to in-person interviews; accordingly, I decided to widen my scope. I designed and distributed a questionnaire to facilitate research among a greater variety of respondents. This questionnaire was anecdotal rather than empirical in nature. That is, it served to collect stories about the respondents' experiences rather than data that I would then quantify with intent to prove or disprove hypotheses. To provide a sense of context for the respondents, however, I asked a variety of questions regarding age, sex, family background, and circumstances of the parents' deaths that resembled questions typical of more empirically oriented questionnaires.

These are the core questions that the questionnaire posed:

Were you responsible for taking care of either or both parents during the time before they died?

Who else had responsibility for your parent's well-being at the time?

What kind of care did your parents need?

Did your parent's death have financial or legal consequences for you? How did these consequences affect your life?

In what ways did your parent's death affect your life? Change it? Disrupt it? Harm it? Improve it? Please explain.

If both of your parents have died, did you feel different after your mother's death than after your father's death? Please explain.

Do you feel that you have "gotten over" your parent's death? If so, how do you feel now? If not, what will have to happen before you have gotten over the death? Please explain.

Did your parent's death change your relationships with other people? With your other parent? With your brothers and sisters? With other relatives? With your spouse? With your children? With your friends? Please explain.

Following your parent's death, did you ever see a psychiatrist, psychologist, clergyman, or other counselor because of how you felt? If so, did counseling make a difference in how you felt? What sort of difference? Please explain.

Have you experienced the loss of other relatives? Friends? Husband or wife? Children? Please specify. Have these losses felt different from the loss of your parent? Please explain.

Other comments?

I distributed 1,084 copies of the questionnaire, initially through hospice organizations but also through universities and other schools; in addition, I distributed copies by word of mouth and by advertising about my research in city and local newspapers. Of the copies distributed, I received 208 back. I decided early on to use only those questionnaires whose respondents were twenty years of age or older at the time of at least one parent's death. The reason for this decision is that the experience of parental loss understandably affects children and adolescents differently from the way it affects adults. I didn't feel prepared or committed to examining these other issues. Moreover, social scientists have more often studied the experience of parental loss for persons under twenty. I therefore didn't use the 25 questionnaires from persons who were twenty or younger when their parents died. This culling left 183 questionnaires in my sample. Of these 183 respondents, 148 were women and 35 were men; they ranged in age from twenty to ninety-four.

Social scientists and clinicians reading *When Parents Die* will note that I haven't analyzed the questionnaires by means of formal empirical methodology. My choice of method was entirely intentional. However, it does not reflect a lack of interest in such a methodology; rather, it's a consequence of my own training and interests. I believe that parental loss is a worthy subject for empirical study, and I urge researchers with an interest in this field to undertake relevant projects. Given the demographics of the United States, "hard" research into parental loss is long overdue.

My third and fourth methods of research involved interviewing prominent psychologists, psychiatrists, sociologists, social workers, and other researchers and clinicians; and, in addition, it involved reading these authorities' papers, books, and published lectures. Most of the interviews took place in person; several were phone interviews; one was an exchange of letters. The people interviewed were:

Rana Binder, M.S.W., St. Vincent's Hospice, New York, NY

John Bowlby, M.D., Tavistock Institute, London, U.K.

Henry Coppolillo, M.D., University of Colorado School of Medicine, Denver, CO

Robert Cowan, M.D., Denver, CO

Jeanne Dennis, M.S.W., Cabrini Hospice, New York, NY

Noreen Dunnigan, M.S., Marin Suicide Prevention Center, San Anselmo, CA

Wendy Foster-Evans, M.S.W., Hospice of Marin, San Rafael, CA

Louise Fradkin, Children of Aging Parents, Levittown, PA

Robert Fulton, Ph.D., Center for Death Education and Research, Minneapolis, MN

Evelyn Gladu, M.Ed., Omega, Boston, MA

Susan Gurbino, M.S.W., Metro Jewish Geriatric Center, Brooklyn, NY

Jane Heald, National Support Center for Families of the Aging, Swarthmore, PA

Herbert Hendin, M.D., Metropolitan Hospital, New York, NY

Lily Ann Hoge, M.S.W., Philadelphia, PA

Carolyn Jaffe, R.N., Hospice of Metro Denver, Denver, CO

Marvin Jaffe, M.D., Denver, CO

Marcia Lattanzi, R.N., M.A., Boulder County Hospice, Boulder, CO

Mirca Liberti, M.Ed., Children of Aging Parents, Levittown, PA

Robert Jay Lifton, M.D., Yale University, New Haven, CT

Miriam Moss, Ph.D., Philadelphia Geriatric Center, Philadelphia, PA

Sidney Z. Moss, M.D., Northwest Community Mental Health Center, Philadelphia, PA

Colin Murray Parkes, M.D., London Medical College, London, U.K.

Carol Pierskalla, Ph.D., National Support Center for Families of the Aging, Swarthmore, PA

Anne Rosberger, M.S.W., Bereavement and Loss Center, New York, NY

Phil Thomsen, Psy.D., Denver, CO

Robert Weiss, Ph.D., Boston University, Boston, MA

Combined, the interviews with these social scientists and the study of their writings allowed me a vastly greater scope in writing *When Parents Die* than I would have had alone. This book may be the product of one pen, but it has its source in many minds.

RESOURCES

There is perhaps no greater source of needless frustration during a family crisis than the sense that you're dealing with it entirely alone. Even the most competent adult can be worn down and demoralized by a feeling of isolation. Fortunately, an increasing number of organizations exist to help you with the problems you face. This increase has occurred despite (or because of?) the decline of state- and federally financed social services in recent years. Admittedly the task of finding and coordinating available resources takes effort and imagination. But you can find help during your time of need.

This section of *When Parents Die* therefore serves to bring possible resources to your attention. I've categorized listings as carefully as possible; however, some of the agencies' purposes or services overlap. Please check the whole list to make sure you aren't missing a good source of help. Also, note that most of these resources are clearinghouses or umbrella organizations. They won't provide direct services to you, but they can inform you of specific agencies or groups that offer such services in your community.

The sad truth is that, given the difficulties facing many adults as their parents age and die, our country still lacks many facilities and services available in less affluent nations. Yet the growing concern about the elderly in America—and the concern about the family members who help the elderly—suggests that our attitudes are changing. The following resources can't provide everything, but they're a good start.

Information on Death and Dying

Center for Death Education and Research
1114 Social Science Building
University of Minnesota
Minneapolis, MN 55455

CDER sells books, pamphlets, and articles about a wide range of subjects pertaining to death and dying. Although many of these publications are most appropriate for mental health professionals, others are intended for a lay audience.

Concern for Dying
250 West 57th Street
New York, NY 10107
(212) 246-6962

This educational organization has been instrumental in promoting the Living Will as a response to indiscriminant use of medical technology in the United States. CFD will provide a free Living Will document in response to mail and telephone inquiries. In addition, CFD provides information on other issues of health care and dying.

The Elisabeth Kübler-Ross Center
South Route 616
Head Waters, VA 24442
(703) 396-3441

As part of her continuing involvement with terminal patients, Dr. Kübler-Ross has established a rural retreat to promote her ideas about health care. The center will provide workshops, seminars, books, and audio and video tapes.

The Foundation of Thanatology
630 West 168th Street
New York, NY 10032

This foundation is an educational and scientific organization intended primarily for health care and mental health care professionals; however, some of its informational services might be helpful to lay people with a strong interest (including personal interest) in thanatology.

Grief Education Institute
2422 South Downing Street
Denver, CO 80210
(303) 777-9234

GEI is fundamentally a regional bereavement counseling agency, but also provides information about death and grief to a wider audience.

Public Affairs Pamphlets
381 Park Avenue South
New York, NY 10016

This organization publishes pamphlets on a wide variety of subjects, among them depression, suicide, care of the aging, and resolution of disputes.

Caring for the Elderly

Children of Aging Parents
2761 Trenton Road
Levittown, PA 19056
(215) 547-1070

CAPS is an organization designed to educate families and friends of the elderly; to disseminate information on aging to the wider community; to provide assistance in starting peer support groups; to compile and publish educational materials; and to present educational in-service training. Available materials include a bibliography, manuals for starting self-help groups, and information sheets on nursing homes, Medicare, financial management, etc.

InterStudy
P.O. Box S
5715 Christmas Lake Road
Excelsior, MN 55331
(612) 474-1176

InterStudy has compiled "information about 152 nationwide programs that provide services geared toward families caring for older members." Although intended for health care and mental health care professionals, InterStudy's 370-page guide may be useful to families. It costs $25 (prepaid). For further information on InterStudy's current activities and publications about aging, write to the above address.

National Council on the Aging, Inc.
600 Maryland Avenue, S.W.
West Wing 100
Washington, DC 20023
(202) 479-1200

The Family Caregivers Program (FCP) of the National Council on the Aging serves primarily to inform professional caregivers about research and resources for the elderly. However, some NCOA materials may be useful to families themselves. Among these publications is *An Idea Book on Caregiver Support Groups*, which includes a list of 300 relevant organizations. Contact Lorraine Lidoff for further information.

National Support Center for Families of the Aging
P.O. Box 245
Swarthmore, PA 19081
(215) 544-5933

Designed "to provide help to families and other caregivers of the elderly," NSCFA offers seminars about caring for aging parents; publishes a newsletter, *Change;* and distributes a series of cassette tapes about understanding and communicating with aging parents. NSCFA will send information about activities upon receipt of a long, self-addressed stamped envelope.

Information About Illnesses

If your parent suffers from one or more diseases, you can obtain information about medical matters and/or available resources from the following national organizations:

Alzheimer's Disease and Related Disorders Association, Inc.
360 North Michigan Avenue
Chicago, IL 60601
(312) 853-3060

American Cancer Society
777 Third Avenue
New York, NY 10036

American Foundation for the Blind
15 West 16th Street
New York, NY 10011
(212) 620-2000

American Heart Association, Inc.
205 East 42nd Street
New York, NY 10017
(212) 661-5335

American Lung Association
1740 Broadway
New York, NY 10019
(212) 315-8700

The Arthritis Foundation
115 East 18th Street
New York, NY 10003
(212) 477-8700

Cancer Care, Inc.
The National Cancer Foundation, Inc.
One Park Avenue
New York, NY 10016
(212) 221-3300

Multiple Sclerosis National Society
205 East 42nd Street
New York, NY 10017
(212) 986-3240

National Kidney Foundation
2 Park Avenue
New York, NY 10016
(212) 889-2210

Stroke Foundation, Inc.
898 Park Avenue
New York, NY 10021
(212) 734-3461

Information About Alcohol and Drug Abuse

National Council on Alcoholism, Inc.
733 Third Avenue
New York, NY 10010
(212) 206-6770

NCA provides information about educational and counseling resources on alcoholism.

Hospice Care

National Hospice Organization
1901 North Fort Myer Drive, Suite 902
Arlington, VA 22209
(703) 243-5900

NHO does not provide direct patient services. However, it publishes a directory of hospice organizations and related services throughout the United States. NHO will provide callers with the names of hospices in their area.

Funerals and Memorial Societies

Continental Association of Funeral and Memorial Societies
1828 L Street, N.W., Suite 1100
Washington, DC 20036

For persons who wish to arrange simple, inexpensive funerals, this organization can be helpful. Check the phone book for a local chapter; otherwise contact the above address for more specific information.

The National Funeral Directors Association
135 West Wells Street
Milwaukee, WI 53203

NFDA supplies a series of pamphlets explaining aspects of funerals, funeral expenses, cremation, and other services of the mortuary industry.

Living Wills and Organ Donation

Concern for Dying
250 West 57th Street
New York, NY 10017
(212) 246-6962

This educational organization has been instrumental in promoting the Living Will as a response to excessive medical technology in the United States. CFD will provide a free Living Will document in response to mail and telephone inquiries. In addition, CFD provides information on other issues of health care and dying.

The Living Bank
P.O. Box 6725
Houston, TX 77265

A nonprofit service organization, The Living Bank is "dedicated to helping those who wish to donate part or all of their bodies for transplantation, therapy, medical research or anatomical studies" after death.

Suicide Prevention and Counseling

American Association of Suicidology
2459 South Ash Street
Denver, CO 80222
(303) 692-0985

AAS can supply information about local resources for survivors of suicide, as well as literature about suicide and its aftermath for families. (Note: AAS is an information clearinghouse, not a crisis center.)

The Life Clinic
1026 South Robertson Boulevard
Los Angeles, CA 90035
(213) 657-6014

Providing a variety of services for suicide prevention and counseling of survivors of suicide, the Life Clinic is one of the pioneering centers of its kind in the United States.

Survivors of Suicide
Suicide Prevention Center
184 Salem Avenue
Dayton, OH 45406
(513) 223-9096

Survivors of Suicide provides information and counseling about suicide; in addition, the group publishes a quarterly newsletter and a resource directory, *Survivors of Suicide Services* (available for $3.00).

Widowhood

Widowed Persons Service
American Association of Retired Persons
1909 K Street, N.W.
Washington, DC 20049
(202) 872-4700

In addition to providing a variety of services to the retired, AARP also sponsors a program called Widowed Persons Service. This service offers one hundred and eighty programs nationwide to newly widowed persons of all ages. AARP provides publications, among them an excellent pamphlet entitled "On Being Alone"; a bibliography on bereavement; film and filmstrip information; and a list of programs for the widowed nationwide. See also additional listing under Other Resources.

Assistance for Women

National Organization for Women
P.O. Box 7813
Washington, DC 20044
(202) 347-2279

As part of its work to achieve women's rights, NOW has concerned itself with issues specifically affecting older women.

Older Women's League
1325 G Street, N.W.
Lower Level
Washington, D.C. 20005
(202) 783-6686

"The Older Women's League is the only national grassroots membership organization whose sole focus is women in the middle years and beyond." Created in 1980, OWL addresses issues such as pension rights, health insurance, caregiver and support services. OWL publishes a newspaper and a series of workbooks for women's midlife planning.

Women's Action Alliance, Inc.
370 Lexington Avenue
New York, NY 10017
(212) 532-8330

"The Alliance's purpose is to develop educational programs and services that assist women and women's organizations to accomplish their goals." Although the Alliance doesn't provide services directly applicable to medical care and bereavement services, it can supply information about agencies that can help women deal with family issues.

Other Resources

American Association of Retired Persons
1909 K Street, N.W.
Washington, DC 20049
(202) 872-4700

AARP provides a wide range of services for the retired. This organization's concerns include medical, financial, educational, and safety issues. In addition, AARP has some of the best information available about resources for widows and widowers. (See also additional listing under Widowhood.)

Money Management Institute
Household International
2700 Sanders Road
Prospect Heights, IL 60070
(312) 564-5000

To provide consumers with information about planning, investment, saving, and other financial issues, Money Management Institute has produced a series of booklets available at a nominal cost.

National Organization for Victim Assistance
1757 Park Road, N.W.
Washington, DC 20010
(202) 232-8560
Twenty-four-hour hotline: (202) 393-6682

NOVA is a private, nonprofit organization providing four services: national advocacy for victims' rights; help for crime victims; service to local programs; and membership support. Among other things, NOVA can help you locate victim assistance resources in your community. NOVA also provides twenty-four-hour telephone crisis counseling for all types of victims.

National Self-Help Clearinghouse
33 West 42nd Street, Room 1227
New York, NY 10036

NSHC "does research on self-help groups, provides training and technical assistance, runs conferences, and publishes a newsletter." To obtain information about self-help groups throughout the United States, send a self-addressed stamped envelope to the above address.

Parents Without Partners, Inc.
7910 Woodmont Avenue
Bethesda, MD 20814
(301) 654-8850

Although this organization may seem tangential to dealing with the death of a parent, its services—"devoted to the welfare and interests of single parents and their children"— could be useful to adults who are attempting to care for their own parents while raising children alone. Services include crisis intervention, seminars, educational meetings, and publications.

FURTHER READING

During the past fifteen years, this country has witnessed an explosion of interest in thanatology. The interest isn't always matched by actual changes in how Americans deal with issues of death and dying, but it suggests at least the potential for change. For the concerned reader—whether bereaved or not—the resources available in libraries and bookstores are encouraging.

What follows is not an inclusive bibliography. It is, however, a selection of books likely to be useful in the aftermath of a parent's death, or during a parent's illness. I've broken the subject down into several categories. Inevitably, there is some overlap of subjects between them. In addition, there is some intentional inconsistency in the listings themselves. I haven't listed the addresses for major publishers; you can locate them easily through any bookstore, or in the Bowker publication *Books in Print*. However, I've indicated how you can reach lesser-known publishers directly. Note, too, that many of the agencies listed in Appendix B publish leaflets or books pertaining to one or more aspects of illness, death, and bereavement.

General

Bernstein, Joanne E. *Loss.* New York: Clarion Books, 1977.
Concise, clear advice on dealing with grief.

Caine, Lynn. *Lifelines.* New York: Doubleday & Co., 1978.
The problem of loneliness and how to overcome it.

Grollman, Earl (ed.). *Concerning Death: A Practical Guide for the Living.* Boston: Beacon Press, 1974.
Comprehensive guide to issues of death and loss.

———. *Living When a Loved One Has Died.* Boston: Beacon Press, 1977.
Reassuring essays about coping with loss.

———. *What Helped Me When My Loved One Died.* Boston: Beacon Press, 1981.
Personal essays about death, loss, and grief.

Henderson, Diane. *Coping with Grief.* Tuscumbia, AL: Henderson Clark Publishers, 1979. Address: P.O. Box 561, Tuscumbia, AL 35674.
Short booklet about the grief process.

Krementz, Jill. *How It Feels When a Parent Dies.* New York: Alfred A. Knopf, 1981.
Stories of bereaved children, with photographs.

Kübler-Ross, Elisabeth. *Death: The Final Stage of Growth.* New York: Macmillan Publishing Co., 1981.
Essays and photo-essays about the dying.

———. *Living with Death and Dying.* New York: Macmillan Publishing Co., 1981.
Essays about various issues of death and dying.

———. *On Death and Dying.* New York: Macmillan Publishing Co., 1969.
Popular work about understanding death and dying.

LeShan, Eda. *Learning to Say Good-by.* New York: Avon, 1976.
Sensitive book for children about parental loss.

Manning, Doug. *Don't Take My Grief Away.* New York: Harper & Row, 1984.
Minister's recommendations about dealing with grief.

Parkes, Colin Murray. *Bereavement: Studies of Grief in Adult Life.* New York: International Universities Press, 1977.
An English psychiatrist's research into grief.

Pinkus, Lily. *Death and the Family.* New York: Vintage Books, 1974.
Family dynamics and bereavement.

Rollin, Betty. *Last Wish.* New York: Linden Press/Simon & Schuster, 1985.
A daughter's story of assisting her mother's suicide.

Shephard, Martin. *Someone You Love Is Dying.* New York: Harper & Row, 1980.
Practical information about loss and grief.

Tatelbaum, Judy. *The Courage to Grieve.* New York: Harper & Row, 1980.
Useful recommendations about dealing with grief.

Temes, Roberta. *Living with an Empty Chair.* Amherst, MA: Mandala, 1977.
Unusually eloquent commentary on loss and grief.

Vail, Elaine. *A Personal Guide to Living with Loss.* New York: John Wiley & Sons, 1982.
Comprehensive treatment, including practical matters.

Technical Literature

Bowlby, John. *Attachment and Loss: Vol. I, Attachment.* New York: Basic Books, 1980.
Detailed study of human attachment behavior.

———. *Attachment and Loss: Vol. II, Anxiety and Anger.* New York: Basic Books, 1980.
Consequences of disrupted attachment in humans.

———. *Attachment and Loss: Vol. III, Loss.* New York: Basic Books, 1980.
Study of bereavement and loss.

Fulton, R. *Death, Grief, and Bereavement: A Bibliography.* New York: Arno Press, 1977. Address: Center for Death Education and Research, 1114 Social Sciences Building, University of Minnesota, Minneapolis, MN 55455.
Annotated bibliography about death and dying.

Furman, Erna. *A Child's Parent Dies.* New Haven, CT: Yale University Press, 1974.
How parental loss affects children.

Garfield, Charles A. *Psychosocial Care of the Dying Patient.* San Francisco: McGraw-Hill Book Co., 1978.
Psychological issues of terminally ill patients.

Gorer, Geoffrey. *Death, Grief and Mourning.* Garden City, NJ: Doubleday & Co., 1965.
Anthropologist's view of death and loss.

Horowitz, Mardi, *et al.* "Initial Psychological Response to Parental Death," in *Archives of General Psychiatry,* vol. 38, March 1981, pp. 316–23.
Comparison of two groups of adults and their reactions to parental loss.

———. "Reactions to the Death of a Parent," in the *Journal of Nervous and Mental Disease,* vol. 172, no. 7, pp. 383–92.

Comparison of two groups of subjects who had suffered the loss of a parent.

Lifton, Robert Jay. *The Life of the Self.* New York, Basic Books, 1983.
Theoretical essays on life and death.

Maguire, Daniel C. *Death by Choice.* Garden City, NY: Image Books, 1984.
Sensitive examination of euthanasia and medical ethics.

Margolis, Otto S., *et al. Acute Grief: Counseling the Bereaved.* New York: Columbia University Press, 1981.
Wide range of essays on issues of acute grief.

Moss, Miriam S., and Sidney Z. Moss. "The Impact of Parental Death on Middle-Aged Children," in *Omega,* vol. 14 (1), 1983–84, pp. 65–75.
Examination of parental loss and its consequences.

Osterweis, Marion, *et al.,* eds. *Bereavement: Reactions, Consequences, and Care.* Washington, D.C.: National Academy Press, 1984.
Compendium of articles about loss and grief.

Owen, Grey, *et al.* "Death at a Distance: A Study of Family Survivors," in *Omega,* vol. 13: 3, 1982–83, pp. 191–225.
Comparison of adult reactions to kinds of loss.

Parkes, Colin Murray, and Robert S. Weiss. *Recovery from Bereavement.* New York: Basic Books, 1983.
Detailed study of widowhood in America and England.

Raphael, Beverley. *The Anatomy of Bereavement.* New York: Basic Books, 1983.
Detailed, inclusive study of all aspects of loss.

Veatch, Robert M. *Death, Dying, and the Biological Revolution.* New Haven, CT: Yale University Press, 1976.
Examination of technology and medical ethics.

Widowhood

American Association of Retired Persons. *On Being Alone.* Long Beach, CA: AARP Widowed Persons Service, 1984. Address: Box 199, Long Beach, CA 90801.
Booklet about adjustment to widowhood.

Antoniak, Helen, *et al. Alone: Emotional, Legal and Financial Help for the Widowed or Divorced Woman.* Millbrae, CA: Les Femmes/Celestial Arts, 1979.
Practical information for widows and divorcees.

Burges, Jane, and Willard Kohn. *The Widower.* Boston: Beacon Press, 1978.
Practical guide for widowers.

Caine, Lynn. *Widow.* New York: Bantam, 1981.
First-person account of widowhood.

Fisher, Ida, and Byron Lane. *The Widow's Guide to Life.* Englewood Cliffs, NJ: Prentice-Hall, 1981.
Comprehensive book for recent widows.

Loewinsohn, Ruth J. *Survival Handbook for Widows.* Chicago: Follett, 1979. Address: c/o New Century, 275 Old New Brunswick Road, Piscataway, NJ 08854.
Concise guide for widows.

Tawes, Isabella. *The Widow's Guide.* New York: Schocken Books, 1981.
Discussions of practical and emotional aspects of widowhood.

Practical Tasks

Bloomfield, Harold H. *Making Peace with Your Parents.* New York: Random House, 1983.
Self-help manual for coping with parental conflict.

Dacey, Norman F. *How to Avoid Probate!* New York: Crown Publishers, 1983.
Guidebook for dealing with estates and probate.

Silverstone, Barbara, and Helen Kandel Hyman. *You and Your Aging Parent.* New York: Pantheon, 1982.
Excellent guidebook for helping and dealing with elderly parents.

Soled, Alex J. *The Essential Guide to Wills, Estates, Trusts, and Death Taxes.* Glenview, IL: Scott, Foresman & Co., 1984.
Q-and-A format manual about legal matters relevant to estates.

Stock, Barbara R. *It's Easy to Avoid Probate and Guardianships.* Orlando, FL: Linch Publishing, 1984. Address: P.O. Box 75, Orlando, FL 32802.
Guidebook for estate planning and setting up guardianships.

Suicide

Hendin, Herbert. *Suicide in America.* New York: Norton, 1982.
Overview of suicide among Americans.

Schneidman, Edwin S., and Norman L. Farberow. *Clues to Suicide.* New York: McGraw-Hill, 1957.
Classic study of suicide.

INDEX